The
Lampshade Lady's Guide
to Lighting Up Your Life

50 *custom*
lampshades
& lamps

Judy Lake with Kathleen Hackett
photography by Ryan Benyi and George Bouret

POTTER
CRAFT

NEW YORK

Published in the United States by Potter Craft,
an imprint of the Crown Publishing Group, a
division of Random House, Inc., New York.
www.clarksonpotter.com
wwww.pottercraft.com

POTTER CRAFT and colophon is a registered
trademark of Random House, Inc.

Library of Congress Cataloging-in-Publication
Data
Lake, Judy.
    The Lampshade Lady's guide to lighting up
your life : 50 custom lampshades and lamps /
Judy Lake with Kathleen Hackett.—1st ed.
        p.   cm.
    Includes index.
    ISBN 978-0-307-45232-0
    1. Lampshades. 2. Lamps. 3. Salvage
(Waste, etc.)   I. Hackett, Kathleen.
    II. Title.   III. Title: Lighting up your life.
    TT897.L32 2009
    745.593'2-dc22
                2008043250

Printed in China

Design by La Tricia Watford
How-to photography and photography
pages 10, 13, 43–45, 127 by George Bouret
All other photography © 2008 by
Ryan Benyi Photography

10 9 8 7 6 5 4 3 2 1
First Edition

contents

introduction

EVERYWHERE I GO I AM CALLED THE LAMPSHADE LADY.

If I go shopping at the supermarket or out to dinner, it's always, "Hey, it's the Lampshade Lady!"

On the beach—from the coast of Maine to the island of Tortola—customers have spotted me and, instead of saying hello, exclaimed, "That was the Lampshade Lady!"

Over the phone, callers greet me not with "Judy Lake, please" but rather, "Have I reached the Lampshade Lady?"

Once, when I was rifling through piles of vintage fabric at an upscale antiques shop in Massachusetts, the proprietor broke the hushed silence by blurting out, "Aren't you that Lampshade Lady?"

Indeed, I am. I don't mind the moniker, especially as I get older and realize how hard it has become to remember anyone's name. The Lampshade Lady works for me, not least because there aren't many of us around. To put it mildly, I am passionate about making lampshades—made out of everything from old-school children's cloth books, vintage fabrics, antique postcards, backcloth, chenille, you name it. In fact, one time I begged a customer to give me the very paisley-print pants she was wearing. You see, for me, lampshades are anything but the afterthought they so often become when one is decorating or redecorating a space. And that's where *The Lampshade Lady's Guide to Lighting Up Your Life* comes in. In this book, I turn the notion that lampshades are an underwhelming piece of the interior design puzzle on its head.

I come by my passion honestly, if not genetically. Grammy Gulian, a world-class knitter and needleworker, was always making someone in the family a new sweater. Grandma Sawyer was educated in the fine arts at the Boston Museum School in the late 1920s. Later, she opened her own studio in Greenwich Village and went on to make coveted cut silver jewelry and boxes. (I still have some pieces!) We were birds of a feather, my grandmothers and me—always working with our hands, creating beautiful things. When I wasn't busy sewing, quilting, spinning wool, or weaving, I was cutting out pretty dresses for my beloved paper dolls.

My first entrepreneurial experience was in the seventh grade, when the macramé craze grabbed hold of me. I made wall hangings and belts by the dozens, which I proudly brought in to show the owner of Benoit's department store in Portland, Maine, where I grew up. My first "trunk show" was a success, as Mr. Benoit bought every single belt I had made. I was a proud little artisan!

Inspired by my grandmothers and fueled by the hundreds of crafts shows my mother took me to throughout high school, I spent my college years studying textile design. I became intensely interested in tapestry weaving and chose to spend a year at Folk High School south of Malmö, Sweden, across the bay from Copenhagen. While I should have been in class, I spent most of my time in the Danish city soaking in its jaw-dropping modern design. It still informs much of what I create.

Leap to 1986, when my husband, Carson, and I moved south from our post-college farmhouse in Waitsfield, Vermont, to Pawlet, a rural community in the farm country of southern Vermont. Carson had been offered a position as sous-chef at the storied Equinox Hotel, a grand landmark in nearby Manchester that had been shuttered for thirteen years. As a young mom at home with a new baby, I was essentially a widow—of the chef's-wife kind—and had a lot of spare time on my very eager hands. So just before my son, Duncan, was born, I taught myself how to make lampshades. Though the little

shop up the road offered classes on making cut-and-pierced-style shades, I convinced the owner that I didn't need a teacher, so she sent me off with the supplies and how-to instructions. All excited, I jumped right in when I got home.

By the time Duncan turned one, I had made lampshades for everyone I knew—my family, friends, neighbors—even the proprietors of the village store. When my close pals began asking for more, my entrepreneurial spirit was stoked yet again, so I did what any artisan living in a rural town does: I signed up for a small craft show in Manchester. On that sunny Saturday afternoon, I wrapped a dozen of my finest shades in beautiful gold tissue, boxed six baskets of plump tomatoes from my garden, and bagged six loaves of freshly baked anadama bread and packed it all into my VW® bus. Better to diversify to maximize profits, I thought. I was nervous, to say the least. The chutzpah that brought me to Benoit's so many years before was replaced with fear.

This was serious business. By four o'clock, I had sold all of the tomatoes, all of the bread, and not a single lampshade. They may not have put money in my pocket, but those shades garnered all the compliments I could have hoped for. Besides, I rationalized, they were expensive for this type of craft show. At $35–$40 each, a lampshade was a far bigger financial commitment than, say, a $3 loaf of bread! I was not deterred. Soon I'd invested in a craft tent, a display table, and fun signs for an upcoming show in Bennington, Vermont. Eventually, show by show, I became savvier about displaying my lampshades and selling them.

Helping customers at craft shows was a tricky business. Most of the time they had no idea what size shade they needed, how it fit on

ABOVE: The Lampshade Lady's shop, a.k.a. Lake's Lampshades, in Pawlet Village, Vermont.

the lamp—with a clip or harp—or how tall the lamp was. Occasionally, an organized customer, usually a designer, would pull out a packet full of swatches and measurements. *Ooh la la!* At last, someone who knew what they needed! And that's when the next entrepreneurial lightbulb went on—why not create a permanent place where people could come with their swatches and lamps, their ideas and questions?

These days you will find me at that place, Lake's Lampshades, my geranium-pink clapboard shop in Pawlet, Vermont. Since 1998 I've been working with customers on choosing just the right fabric and shade to suit their lamps. From the moment I moved in, working with customers became much easier. They call ahead, bring their lamps and fabrics to me, and we solve their tricky lighting issues. I help them choose among the hundreds of options brimming from the shelves and stacks in my space; we first begin with the fabric, which then usually determines the style and shape of the shade. Though I have hundreds of finished shades on hand, much of the work I do is custom, since my customer is design-savvy and often brings in fabric that matches his or her decor.

It's been eleven years since I set up shop, but I'm just as excited today about making lampshades as I was that day I began cutting and piercing almost two decades ago. I also have a burning desire to share my passion with the masses, which is why I offer seasonal classes at my shop and talk about my latest projects, fabric finds, and resources on my website, lakeslampshades.com. Even so, there are thousands more DIYers out there to go! After all, no purchased lampshade ever brings the satisfaction one made by hand does. In this age of mass-produced everything, the beauty and personal value of any one-of-a-kind item grows exponentially, as "personal touch" becomes less and less the norm.

In *The Lampshade Lady's Guide to Lighting Up Your Life,* I share twenty years of lampshade-making experience through more than fifty irresistible projects suited for first-timers as well as those who have already made a shade or two. They range from simple night-lights a child can make to more elaborate, embellished shades that would make any interior decorator swoon. What they all have in common, though, is the ability to transform a room and give it a personal stamp. My goal is for readers to realize just how important a well-dressed lamp is to a decorating scheme. But most importantly, I hope they come away from a completed project as happy as I do when I glue on that last piece of trim. My other wish? It's that if readers ever run into me, they will feel comfortable marching right up to me and gleefully saying, "Hey, you're the Lampshade Lady!" And perhaps, inspired by my story, they'll consider starting a craft business of their own.

The Language of Lampshade Making

The lighting industry has undergone a major fashion trajectory, having made huge strides in the past decade far beyond the pleated, plastic-covered lampshades that defined Aunt Ethel's dream living room. Now, lighting has become as integral to a room's design as a sofa, rug, or fireplace surround. Still, I overhear customers in my shop say that they will return to pick out lampshades once the room is done. I have to bite my tongue! Why not order an extra yard or two of drapery fabric to make a pair of lampshades?

The options for custom-designed lampshades (that you can make yourself!) are infinite. An oversized drum shade hanging in the entryway announces a home unlike any other decorative element, as does a pair of shades hanging over the dining room table. Do it with a bright, colorful lamp topped with a matching shade or a pretty, hand-blown glass base crowned with a shade covered in vintage French ticking. What's more, unlike committing to a fabric for an upholstered sofa, putting cloth on a lampshade is a relatively small commitment.

LAMPSHADE SHAPES

Hard-back lampshades, those that feature fabric or paper laminated to pressure-sensitive styrene, are available in a wonderful array of styles and sizes. They are perfect for use with vintage textiles, since they fare far better when laminated than when sewn into soft-sided shades. What's more, there is little more than fabric, scissors, and glue involved in putting them together—no sewing necessary! Below are the shades you'll find in this book.

DRUM SHADES are, well, drum shaped. They are equal in width on the top and bottom. A hanging, or pendant, drum shade is made with either a washer top or an uno-top wire and is suspended on a wire or cord. The secret to using a pendant drum shade to its best advantage is to hang it so that the lightbulb does not shine directly into your face; a diffuser can be fitted onto the bottom of the hanging drum shade to alleviate this problem. I am the first one to break this rule, of course, by hanging one over my desk as a task light! In the winter, I use a full-spectrum bulb to prolong the scarce daylight.

However you choose to use a drum shade, it will always make a graphic statement in a room. The drum shape will forever be reminiscent of the '50s, but it also fits beautifully into a contemporary minimalist interior because it can handle both bold prints and calming neutrals. Drum shades are among the easiest to make and can be cut into any size.

EMPIRE SHADES are perhaps the most ubiquitous shade. I am willing to bet that there is at least one in your home. An empire shade is cone-shaped, but the slant is gradual. The shades can feature a clip, washer, hurricane, or uno-top and a bottom ring. You might think about empire shades as the little black dress of the lampshade lineup—they are versatile, always correct, and can be dressed up or down depending on the fabric and lamp base you choose. Empire shades look especially attractive on round bases. In fact, this is my choice whenever a customer brings me a spherical base.

A caveat: Stay away from horizontal stripes for this shade; it is difficult to get the lines to look straight. I always advise customers to bring in their old empire shade so that I can use it as a pattern for a new shade, as in the Recovered Empire Shade on page 26.

HEXAGONAL FRAMES are six-sided shades that come in a host of sizes and variations. With so many sizes to choose from, it can be confusing to pair the right size hexagonal shade with a particular lamp. I find the easiest way is to find the right height first, then play with different bottom widths and finally strike the right top width. Hexagonal shades are measured from one corner to the opposite corner for the top and bottom dimensions. The height is measured on the slant from top to bottom.

HEXAGONAL BELL SHADES flair at the bottom, giving them a more feminine look. They, too, are available in sizes as small as a candelabra shade; the largest available is 16" (40.5cm) across and 12" (30.5cm) high.

Both hexagonals and hexagonal bell shapes are fitting for country and traditional settings and make the perfect toppers for ginger-jar lamps, pear-shaped lamps, glass kerosene lamps, and Depression glass lamps. I am partial to using toile and stripes on hexagonal and hexagonal bell shades, since these patterns are not compromised by the shape and fit nicely into the panels.

HEXAGONAL SCALLOP FRAMES feature bottoms in which the panels are scalloped, or rounded. They are available in sizes as small as a candelabra shade up to 14" (35.5cm) across the bottom. Scallop shades marry well with round

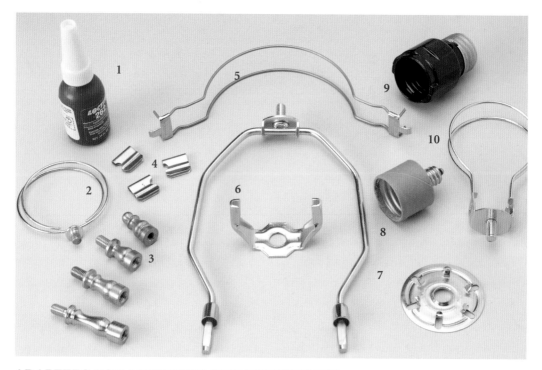

ADAPTERS FOR ACHIEVING THE PERFECT FIT

1. threadlocker, such as Loctite® brand
2. flush clip adapter
3. grouping of shade risers
4. brass clips to hold shade snug against glass diffuser
5. clip adaptor
6. harp and harp wings
7. uno adaptor
8. socket enlarger
9. shade riser
10. clip adapter

lamp bases because the shape of the scallop follows the shape of the base. I am particularly fond of the small hexagonal scallop clip shade on a small stick lamp, as in the Antique Quilt Top Scalloped Shade, page 114. I also choose this shape when I am using textiles like monograms or embroideries that have designs in a corner, which are hard to incorporate with other panel shapes. I suggest you make a hexagonal scallop shade after you've become comfortable with the basic hexagonal shade and other straight-sided styles.

NIGHT-LIGHTS are really half shades mounted on wire frames that are available in hexagonal, triangular, round, and rectangular shapes. Night-lights are among the easiest of shades to make and are perfect for crafting with children. They are available in kits that include all of the fixtures needed to complete the shade (Resources, page 156).

FOUR-SIDED RECTANGULAR FRAMES, a favorite among my clients, are ideal for medium to large lamp bases and look especially good when covered with contemporary fabric. On the other hand, some vintage pieces, such as embroideries, are shaped in such a way that best suits a rectangle, as in the vintage Early Redwork Embroidery Shade, page 104. I like to strike a rather graphic note with the rectangle shade by setting it on a rectangular base, as in the Cool Cottage Flowers Shade, page 60. Small rectangles are a good choice for wall sconces if space is limited, since they can sit almost flush against the wall. All rectangle shades are measured from side to side for the top and bottom dimensions and from top to bottom on the slant for the height.

CUT-CORNER RECTANGULAR SHADES feature eight panels, the corner panels much narrower than those on the front, back, and sides. The additional panels give the shade a rather formal air no matter which fabric is used, whether it's a textured linen or French ticking.

CUT-CORNER RECTANGULAR BELL SHADES are cut-corner rectangles with flair. I choose this shape when I want to highlight a special embroidery or needlepoint piece, especially if there is only enough of it to cover the front panel. I then cover the remaining panels with a neutral fabric.

SQUARE FRAMES have four equal sides and are available in candelabra, clip, and washer-top styles. This shade lends a contemporary feeling to a room, and the expanse of the panels makes them ideal for fabrics with large patterns. Square shades are always measured from side to side and from top to bottom on the slant.

The SQUARE BELL is flared at the bottom to create a bell shape and is the frame I grab for shades for my own home; I love the clean lines, and it suits many a base. It's great for floor lamps, stick lamps, and tall Depression glass lamps. They come in a variety of sizes, from a small candelabra top to larger washer-top frames. The small candle-clip style is very handy for chandeliers and wall sconces.

CUT-CORNER SQUARE and CUT-CORNER SQUARE BELL SHADES are created using eight-sided frames, with narrow, flared panel shapes at each corner. I love to use this frame on alabaster and marble lamp bases. It is the shade I go to when space is an issue. Though it is compact, it has presence.

Cut-corner squares and cut-corner square bells are wonderful showcases for classic decorator fabrics, such as paisley, toile, and formal florals. A needlepoint, such as that on the English Equestrian Needlepoint Shade, page 124, is a perfect choice for a cut-corner square shade.

A WORD ABOUT FABRICS AND TRIMS

To my mind, practically any textile can become a lampshade, whether it's a cast-off couture dress, Grandma's pretty hankie, or a half-finished needlepoint. And then there's the avalanche of fabulous decorator fabrics that are now available. I am partial to time-less fabric designs—after all, it's nice to think of my lampshades as future heirlooms—though I'm not above falling for a color trend or two. Plus it's a far smaller commitment than, say, reupholstering your sofa. That said, I am always trying to push design boundaries by applying vintage textiles to contemporary shades and vice versa. Often the overall look is dominated by the textile, other times by the shade shape, and sometimes by a combination of the two. Choosing the fabrics, shade shapes, and trims is my favorite part of lampshade designing. I keep the options open and ask the questions: Do they work together? Is it too over the top? Is it too forced? Clichéd? Or drop-dead gorgeous?

While I consider the options for covering shades unlimited, I do approach the process thoughtfully. When it comes to working with fabrics, there are a few guidelines:

- Consider the size of the fabric's motif. Small shades do not showcase big prints well, and likewise, big shades look silly with tiny prints. If you love a large print but need a small shade, capture the parts of the design you love best and use them on the panels. When all else fails, let the fabric dictate the size of the lamp!

- Cottons and linens laminate best. They also make the nicest self-trims. Synthetic fabrics often require the use of spray adhesive or a glue gun to achieve proper lamination.

- Vintage fabrics hold a special place in my heart. I take care to cut into only those that wouldn't otherwise be coveted by textile historians or decorative arts museums. In other words, very important vintage textiles should be preserved. Chances are these won't turn up in places like flea markets or tag sales. Nevertheless, if you've unearthed a cache of pieces in the attic, make sure they're not of a particular and irreplaceable provenance. Hard-back shades like the ones in this book are great for preserving very old, fragile textiles. The styrene stabilizes the fabric and saves it from ruin.

- Always wash and dry fabric, whether vintage or new, before using. This will remove some of the sizing and deep creases in new fabric and possibly stains in vintage fabrics. Take care with more fragile pieces by hand-washing them in a gentle soap. If washing doesn't remove creases, use a hot iron. If this doesn't work, cut around them; they will show up as wrinkles in your shade.

- Always hold vintage fabrics up to the light to detect moth holes, subtle stains, or fabric pulls. These will all show up glaringly on a lampshade when the light is turned on. Of course, if you can work a shade around these flaws, by all means, use the fabric.

- Consider the lampshade's purpose when choosing fabric. Warm oranges, reds, and yellows throw nice light for reading. Dark colors, such as black, charcoal gray, navy, and brown, are best used for accent light only.

- The right trim can make or break a shade. Experiment with a number of them before committing to one (or two or three if using a variety for the ribs, top, and bottom trims). You can custom-make self-trims with either the same fabric used for the shade or a complementary fabric. The number of purchased and vintage trims available is unlimited; have fun seeking them out and trying them on your shades.

- Soft cottons are best for self-trims. They are easier to work with than stiff canvas or synthetics. These heavier or more slippery fabrics often require sturdier glue, such as that used with a hot glue gun. They can also be bulky, resulting in a less professional-looking shade.

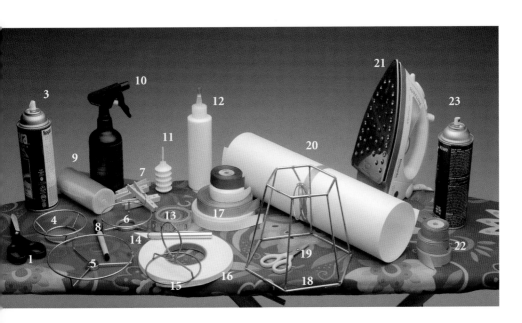

BASIC LAMPSHADE-MAKING SUPPLIES

1. large scissors	8. ultra-thin permanent marker	14. utility knife	19. small scissors
2. work mat		15. clip top	20. pressure-sensitive styrene
3. starch	9. shade wrap	16. pressure-sensitive cloth tape	
4. hurricane-top wire	10. spray bottle		21. iron
	11. squeeze bottle	17. grosgrain ribbon	22. ironing board
5. washer-top wire	12. quick glue		23. spray adhesive
6. uno-top wire	13. tape measure	18. lampshade frame	
7. clothespins			

Basic Lampshade-Making Technique

materials

fabric, cotton or linen

galvanized wire frame of your choice (if using a steel frame, coat with enamel first)

pressure-sensitive styrene for panels, quantity will vary by project

$5/8$"- (16mm-) wide grosgrain ribbon in cotton/rayon blend for trim, quantity will vary by project

pressure-sensitive cloth tape (bias-trim backer)

basic lampshade-making supplies

3 yd (2.75m) $5/8$"- (16mm-) wide grosgrain ribbon to hold panels as they dry

quick glue in squeeze bottle (Glossary, page 154)

scissors

ultra-thin permanent marker

wood clothespins

self-healing mat or quilter's cutting board

iron

ironing board

tape measure

Cut Out the Styrene

[1] Place the styrene sheet on a clean work surface. Lay the shade frame on its side on top of the styrene and roughly trace around the side with the permanent marker. If you are making bell-shaped panels, lay the shade frame on its side, clip the styrene to it with the clothespins, and with one hand behind the styrene, place pressure against the frame while tracing around it. Using the marker lines as your guide, cut out the panel, adding about ½" (13mm) on all sides. This measurement does not need to be exact. You will precisely mark and cut out your panels in step 3.

[2] Clip the panel to the frame at the top and bottom with two clothespins.

[3] Using the marker, mark the styrene along the exterior of the frame panel. This will give you a more precise measure of the panel. Cut out.

[4] Using the cut panel as your template, trace the number of panels needed for your shade onto the styrene. Cut out and set aside.

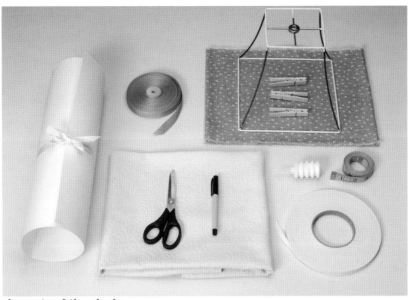

elements of the shade

steps 1–3

steps 4–8

Create the Fabric and Styrene Panels

[5] With the fabric wrong side up, iron it so that it is wrinkle free. Trim away any loose threads or carried threads on crewelwork, embroideries, quilt tops, and needlepoints.

[6] Turn the fabric right side up and place it on a clean work surface. If it is a patterned fabric, study the possibilities for placing the design on your shade. If it has a monogram, chances are you will want it to appear on the front of the shade, either in the center or at the center top or center bottom.

[7] Turn the fabric over so that it is wrong side up. Working with one panel at a time, remove the paper backing from the styrene and place the styrene panel on the back of the fabric as desired. Press with your hand to adhere. Do not iron; the styrene will melt. Flip the fabric over and look at it from the front to make sure your design is where you intended it to be. Cut out the fabric around the styrene panel.

[8] Repeat with the remaining panels of styrene and fabric.

Secure the Panels to the Frame

[9] Place the frame on a work surface. Find the solder mark on the bottom rim of the frame. Start here when recutting to fit your first fabric-covered panel. You may need to work and rework the panel several times, depending on the shade. Those with flared panels such as the hexagonal bell and scallop shades require a bit more patience! Place the panel on the frame and secure with clothespins. Trim the styrene so that it just meets the frame on all sides. Remove it from the frame and mark it with a very tiny number 1 on the back at the bottom. (Don't make the number large, or it will show through your shade when it's lit; the trim will cover a tiny mark.)

[10] Working clockwise around the frame, refit and recut each panel, securing it to the frame with clothespins and marking it with a number as you go.

[11] Beginning with the soldered side of the frame, run a very light bead of glue around this section of the frame, along the top, bottom, and sides. Set the fabric/styrene panel

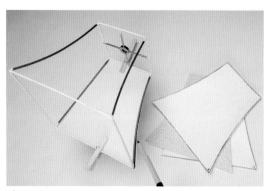

steps 9–10

step 12

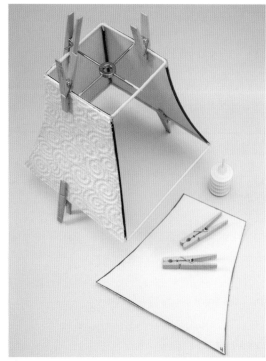

step 11

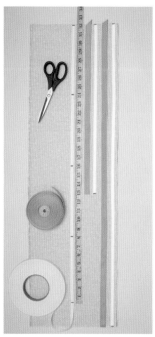

steps 13–15

numbered 1 in place and clip with a clothespin on the top and bottom. Continue affixing the panels to the frame in this fashion, working clockwise and in the order of the numbered panels.

[12] Using the grosgrain ribbon from your basic lampshade-making supplies, tuck one end into a top clothespin on the outside of the shade, pull the ribbon taut, wrap it around to the other side of the shade and secure with the bottom clothespin. Continue wrapping and securing with the ribbon until the panels are held securely in place. Readjust the panels as necessary; straighten and smooth them so that they are positioned properly on the frame. On small shades, only 1 or 2 clothespins per panel are necessary. Set the shade aside to dry for at least 20 minutes.

Make the Trims

[13] Whether using pre-made or self-trims, I always use grosgrain ribbon on the top and bottom of the shade to secure the panels to the wires. Cut 2 lengths of the grosgrain ribbon, each 1" (2.5cm) longer than the circumference of the top and bottom of the shade. If making self-trims instead of buying pre-made trims, for the top and bottom of the shade, cut 2 lengths of the pressure sensitive cloth tape in lengths equal to the strips of grosgrain ribbon. If you're making self-trim for the vertical ribs, which are the wire uprights on the shade, cut one strip of cloth tape for each rib on the shade equal to the height of the shade. Alternatively, cut ⅜"- (9mm-) wide grosgrain or pre-made decorative trim accordingly.

[14] To make the self-trim, place the fabric wrong side up on a work surface. Lay the strips of cloth tape on the fabric. Cut out the strips, adding ¼" (6mm) on each side of the cloth tape and cutting flush to the tape on the ends. Make the self-trims no more than 10 to 15 minutes before putting them on the shade; they'll stiffen if you make them too far in advance.

[15] Working with one strip at a time, apply 2 beads of glue down the exposed length of one side of the fabric, and fold onto the cloth tape. Apply pressure with your hands to smooth out any bumps and to create a crisp edge. Repeat on the other side. Make the remaining trim in this fashion. Take care not to leave excess glue on the trim; wipe it away as you work.

Attach the Trims

[16] When the lampshade has dried, remove the grosgrain and clothespins. Trim away any excess styrene on the top and bottom of shade.

[17] Working on one vertical rib at a time, fold the self-trim or pre-made trim in half lengthwise, wrong sides together, to create a valley. Apply glue in the valley and affix the trim along one of the ribs on the shade. Do not apply so much glue that it oozes out; use your fingernail to remove excess glue from the shade. Repeat with the remaining pieces of rib trim.

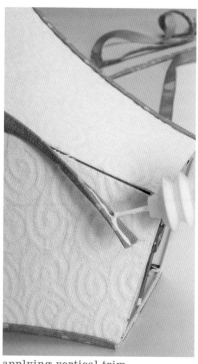

step 16

step 17

applying vertical trim

[18] Attach grosgrain to the bottom rim of the shade to cover the wire frame: Beginning at the solder mark on the bottom of the frame and working a few inches at a time, apply some glue along the bottom edge of the panel. Position the grosgrain so that if you folded it in half lengthwise, the crease that would result could run along the bottom edge of the shade. Use the clothespins to secure the grosgrain as you work. Continue working around the frame, gluing, affixing, and securing, while keeping the grosgrain straight and avoiding over-applying the glue. Trim the ends of the grosgrain on a diagonal so that they overlap just slightly. Apply a bit of glue to the bottom piece of grosgrain and secure the top piece to it, pressing with your hands.

[19] Apply some glue to the back side of the exposed grosgrain, then turn it under so that it wraps around the bottom of the frame, and hand-press to adhere it to the underside of the shade. Use a fingernail to set it snugly against the wire.

[20] Affix the grosgrain to the top of the shade in the same fashion, snipping into the ribbon where it meets the clip top or washer and folding the ribbon over the frame onto its underside.

[21] To apply the self-trims or premade trims to the top and bottom of the shade, work with 3" (7.5cm) of the trim at a time and begin at the center of the panel you have designated to be the back of the shade. Apply glue to the trim and affix directly over the grosgrain from steps 18–20. Be careful not to apply too much glue. Scrape any excess away immediately. You may use clothespins to secure the trim in place, but do not leave them on too long or they may make an indentation on the trim. Cut the ends of trim that meet on the diagonal so that they slightly overlap, and adhere with glue.

TIPS: Shades are measured differently according to their shape but the dimensions are always listed in the same order—top x bottom x height. The top and bottom of square shades are measured from side to side, rectangular shades by the length of the long side x the length of the short side, hexagonal shades from corner to opposite corner, round shades by diameter, and oval shades by the diameter at the widest point. Height should be measured along the ribs or slant of the shade frame.

• If you became overzealous while trimming the panels—oops, now one is too small—there are ways to remedy the situation. In some instances, the fabric can be removed from the panel, but when it can't, there's still hope. Relaminate the panel onto a second piece of styrene that is slightly bigger. Use a panel that fits well as a template and trace around it onto the relaminated panel. Cut out. Secure to the frame with the clothespins and trim carefully to fit.

• As a way to identify your starting point when fitting the panels to the frame, use the solder mark on the bottom of frame. This will help you to keep the panels in order as you assemble the shade.

• If the fabric has a grain, make sure the grain is going in the same direction on all panels. Silk fabrics typically do not laminate well unless they are very textured. Cottons and linens work best.

• Self-trim can be made with the same fabric as the lampshade, or with contrasting fabric, braiding, or gimp. Always wipe away excess glue as you work.

• If you're using vintage fabrics, watch out for spots and/or holes. So many times I haven't noticed them until it was too late!

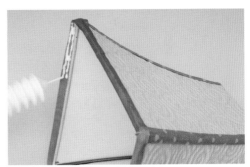
step 19

step 18

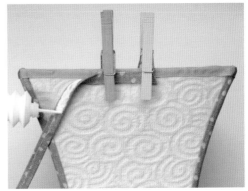
step 21

SIZE MATTERS: Getting the Right Fit

Marrying the right lampshade to the right base can be a challenge, but if you know a bit of basic information, you can strike it right almost every time. That said, once you know the rules, you may by all means break them to satisfy a personal preference, which is something I do all the time. Who says you can't put an enormous drum shade on a rail-thin base? If it looks good to your eye, then go for it. There is one big no-no, however, that should never be compromised: The socket should *never* show when the shade is properly fitted onto the lamp base and the lamp is then placed in a room. Consider the height of the table, bureau, or other surface on which the lamp will be placed, then take stock of where people will be sitting in the room. Will they be looking at the socket when they glance at the lamp?

Here are a few more points to keep in mind regarding fit:

- In general, the size of the lampshade should be proportional to the size of the lamp. To figure out the actual dimensions, use the following guidelines: The height of the shade should be around ⅝ the height of the lamp base when measured from the bottom of the base to the bottom of the light socket. Conventional wisdom is that the diameter of the bottom of the shade should also be close to the height of the lamp. When I measure for a shade, I typically choose one in which the shade's bottom diameter is about 3 inches (7.5cm) wider than the widest part of the base. A small desk lamp, for example, might feature a shade that extends 1" (2.5cm) to 1½" (3.8cm) beyond each side of the lamp base. A shade on a typical floor lamp, on the other hand, would extend from 3" (7.5cm) to as much as 6" (15cm) beyond each side of the base.

- Heavy lamp bases such as jugs or crocks often look better topped with shades that are relatively wide at the top, such as drums, squares, rectangles, or ovals.

- Delicate bases, such as boudoir lamps, fare best with shades in which the top dimensions are smaller than the bottom of the shade, as in coolie and empire styles.

- Take cues from the base shape when choosing a shade. If a lamp has a square or rectangular base, a similarly shaped shade would look great on it. For example, a decoy lamp, which is usually rectangular, always looks marvelous with a rectangular shade. A modernist square base can handle the graphic lines of a square shade.

easy shades

finished measurements

All materials are for a drum shade measuring 12" (30.5cm) across the top x 12" (30.5cm) across the bottom x 8" (20.5cm) high. Adjust according to the size of your shade.

materials

½ yd (46cm) fabric if cutting across selvedge or 1½ yd (1.4m) if the pattern runs vertically up the bolt

12" (30.5cm) washer top

12" (30.5cm) bottom ring

½ yd (46cm) pressure-sensitive styrene

3 yd (2.75m) ⅝"- (16mm-) wide cotton/rayon grosgrain ribbon, for trim

3 yd (2.75m) ¼"- or ⁵⁄₁₆"- (6mm- or 8mm-) wide pressure-sensitive cloth tape (bias-trim backer) for self-trim, if making, or an equal amount decorative trim

yardstick

back seam clamp, optional

basic lampshade-making supplies (page 14)

Funky Drum Shade

It took a little while for my taste to adjust to the style of the drum shade, but now I love them. They're not too difficult to make, and the options for using them are seemingly endless. They work beautifully on modern bases and on end table lamps, floor lamps, and hanging lamps over a dining room table. You can make any size you want as long as you find the right size washer tops. The largest I've found is 18" (45.5cm) (Resources, page 156)—any larger and you need to order them custom made.

It is critical to choose fabrics that laminate easily, since a drum shade requires quite an expanse of fabric and every ripple shows up. Stay away from silk, cotton sheeting, and inexpensive quilting cottons. The fabric I chose here is not a hearty cotton or linen, both of which work best, but I couldn't resist my friend textile designer Susan Sargent's (Resources, page 156) fantastic fabric, which laminated beautifully, perhaps because it was very textured.

TIP: If you want to make a pendant-style light with a drum shade, you can do so using an uno-top or washer-top fixture (Glossary, page 154).

As simple as it looks to make this shade, it is easy to set the wires off center. Getting it right means being very precise when adhering the top and bottom wires onto the arc of styrene. I've been off many times over the years by just a hair, but even that much looks obvious on a shade of this shape. You can use a back seam clamp, available from lampshade supply stores (Resources, page 156) to secure the back seam, but it is not necessary. I find it comes in handy when a shade has a particularly sharp slant.

[1] Prepare a hot iron. On a clean work surface, place the styrene paper side up. You will be making a long rectangle on the styrene. To determine the dimensions to mark on the styrene, multiply the diameter of the shade by 3.14 and add 1" (2.5cm). In this case, it is 12" (30.5cm) x 3.14 + 1" (2.5cm) = 39" (98cm). Using a yardstick laid flush against the left edge of the styrene, mark the styrene with a straight 39" (98cm) long line.

[2] Place the yardstick perpendicular to the line and mark the styrene 8" (20.5cm) for the height of the shade. Mark this same measure at several points along the length of the line. Using the yardstick, connect the marks to make a 39" (98cm) line that is parallel to the one below it. Use the yardstick to close both ends of the parallel lines to make a rectangle. Cut out.

[3] With the wrong side facing you, iron the fabric. With the fabric right side up on a clean work surface, determine where you want the pattern or print to fall onto the shade, if using a patterned fabric. When you have determined where you want the design on the fabric to appear on your shade, turn the fabric over so that it the wrong side is facing you.

[4] Pull the paper backing off the styrene and laminate it to the back of the fabric. Press with your hand to adhere. Do not iron or the styrene will melt. Flip the fabric over and look at it from the front to make sure your design is where you intended it to be. Hand-press to remove any air bubbles. Cut out.

[5] Run a medium-weight bead of glue along the length of the top edge of the back side of the panel. Set the washer top onto the glue along the length of the top edge, securing it with clothespins as you go. You may have to adjust unruly clothespins. I always do!

[6] Flip the shade upside down and set in the bottom wire. Secure with clothespins.

elements of the shade

steps 1-4

steps 5-7

step 9

[7] Glue the back seam together by pulling the panel apart a little bit. Run a couple of beads of glue along the inside seam. Press closed by running your fingers along the seam. Watch out for messy glue on the fabric. Hand-press by running your fingers along the seam, or secure it with the back seam clamp, if you're using one. Set aside to dry, about 20 minutes. When the shade is dry, remove the clothespins and trim the top and bottom of the shade of any excess styrene.

[8] Make the self-trims following steps 13–15 of the Basic Lampshade-Making Technique, page 17. The fabric for my shade has two sides: The darker side is great for the shade itself, whereas the reverse side makes excellent self-trim. Not all fabrics have two sides, but when they do, use them in this way for a shade with perfectly complementary elements.

[9] Add the grosgrain to the top and bottom of the shade followed by the self-trim, following steps 18–21 of the Basic Lampshade-Making Technique, page 18.

finished measurement

All materials are for an empire shade measuring 4" (10cm) across the top x 10" (25.5cm) across the bottom x 7" (18cm) high. Adjust according to the size of your shade.

materials

½ yd (46cm) fabric of your choice

old empire shade

½ yd (46cm) pressure-sensitive styrene

1½ yd (1.4m) ⅝" (15.9mm) cotton/rayon grosgrain ribbon, for trim

2 yd (1.8m) ¼"- or ⁵⁄₁₆"- (6mm- or 8mm-) wide pressure-sensitive cloth tape (bias-trim backer)

⅛ yd (11cm) contrasting fabric for trim

utility knife with #11 blade

masking tape, if necessary

basic lampshade-making supplies (page 14)

Recovered Empire Shade

This is a handy—and inexpensive—way to remake an existing shade that doesn't suit your style anymore.

Gluing the wires to the shade is an awkward business, and it may take you several tries to get it right. Even if the wires are off center only slightly, you'll end up with a lopsided shade. Don't despair—once you successfully make one of these shades, it comes quite easily. In fact, I am willing to bet you'll want to rehabilitate every shade in the house. This shade features a top fitting known a no-thread uno. It is particularly helpful in fitting small round shades because it allows the shade to sit lower on the lamp.

elements of the shade

[1] Carefully remove the old shade from the frame using the utility knife to separate the top and bottom wires from the shade. Try to be as precise as possible, since the old shade will serve as a template for the new shade. Work your way around the shade, sliding the knife along the wires as you go. Pull the lampshade wire out carefully; avoid tearing the shade. If you do tear it, mend it with masking tape. If you can, take apart the back seam. If this isn't possible, cut the shade along the seam.

[2] On a clean work surface, place the old shade onto the pressure-sensitive styrene and trace around it using the permanent marker. If you had to cut the shade up the back, add 1" (2.5cm) to the end of the shade. Cut out.

[3] Turn the fabric right side up and place on a clean work surface. If it is a patterned fabric, study the possibilities for placing the design on your shade. When you have determined where you want the designs on the fabric to appear on your shade, turn the fabric over so that it is wrong side up.

[4] Remove the paper backing from the styrene and place the styrene on the back of the fabric. Press with your hand to adhere. Do not iron; the styrene will melt. Flip the fabric over and look at it from the front to make sure the design is where you intended it to be. Cut out. Hand-press to smooth out the fabric.

steps 1–4

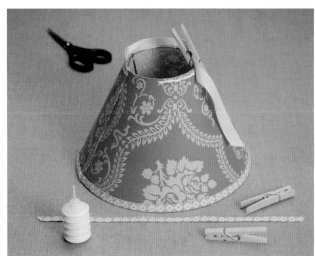

step 9

[5] Run a light bead of glue around the inside top edge of the shade. Set the top wire onto the glue, making sure it is flush with the edge and using clothespins to hold it in place as you work around the shade. Overlap the sides at the back and secure with clothespins.

[6] Turn the shade upside down so that the bottom is facing up. Set the bottom ring in place, flush to the bottom edge of the shade, and secure it with clothespins. Remove clothespins until there are only 6 holding the wire in place. Run a bead of glue around the shade on the inside of the wire.

[7] To close the back seam, lift the overlapping layer back, then run a few beads of glue on the inside of the top layer of the back seam. Smooth with the tip of the squeeze bottle. Turn the shade on its side and hand-press the back seam closed. Wipe away excess glue with your finger.

[8] Prepare the trims while the shade dries, following steps 13–15 of the Basic Lampshade-Making Technique, page 17. Once the shade is dry, remove clothespins and trim away any excess styrene.

[9] Add the grosgrain to the top and bottom of the shade followed by the self-trim, following steps 18–21 of the Basic Lampshade-Making Technique, page 18.

TIP: Once the glue has begun to dry, hand-press the back seam again to ensure a secure seam.

finished measurements

All materials are for a hexagonal clip shade measuring 5" (12.5cm) across the top x 8" (20.5cm) across the bottom x 6" (15cm) high.

materials

6 baseball cards

5" x 8" x 6" (12.5cm x 20.5cm x 15cm) hexagonal clip lampshade frame

½ yd (46cm) pressure-sensitive styrene

1¼ yd (1.1m) ⅝"- (16mm-) wide cotton/rayon grosgrain ribbon to trim the top and bottom of the shade

2¼ yd (2m) ⅜"- (9mm-) wide cotton/rayon grosgrain ribbon in contrasting color, cut into six 6" (15cm) lengths to trim the vertical ribs; the remaining for the top or bottom of the shade

basic lampshade-making supplies (page 14)

Favorite Baseball Cards Shade

This is a fun way not only to put your child's beloved baseball players on display in his or her room, but to include your Little Leaguer on his or her own lampshade. In most junior baseball leagues, players have their photos taken as a team as well as individually and have it printed on a baseball card complete with their statistics, just like the pros. For this project I have included a personal card plus five more of favorite pro players.

The addition of a second piece of grosgrain is not necessary, but it is a great way to make your shade look professional—it helps to straighten the main piece of grosgrain. You can also add soutache or another fun trim in place of the second piece of grosgrain.

step 1

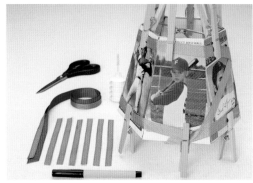
steps 2–4

step 7

[1] Photocopy or scan the baseball cards, enlarging them to 160% or to fit the panels, on the best-quality copier or printer available.

[2] To make a template for the panels, cut out a piece of styrene just slightly bigger than a panel on the frame. Clip it to the top and bottom of the frame with clothespins. Using an ultra-thin permanent marker, trace around the panel onto the styrene. Cut out the panel.

[3] Working with one photocopy at a time, place the template onto it and trace around the template with the permanent marker. Cut out. Repeat with the remaining copies.

[4] Laminate each prepared photocopy to the styrene and cut out. Place the panels in a pile in the order that you want to arrange them on the shade. Follow steps 9–12 of the Basic Lampshade-Making Technique, pages 16–17.

[5] Carefully take the ribbon and clothespins off the shade when it is dry; it is very easy to rip the paper.

[6] Add the 6" (15cm) lengths of ⅜"- (9mm-) wide grosgrain to the vertical ribs. Apply a continuous bead of glue to the grosgrain and set on the shade. Press the grosgrain onto the rib with your fingers to seal firmly. Remove any excess glue with your fingertip. Continue with the remaining strips.

[7] To add grosgrain around the top and bottom of the shade, follow steps 18–20 in the Basic Lampshade-Making Technique, page 18, using the ⅝"- (16mm-) wide grosgrain. If using the ⅜"- (9mm-) wide grosgrain on top of the ⅝"- (16mm-) wide grosgrain, set it on top of the wider one so that about ⅛" (3mm) of the wider one is showing.

finished measurements

All materials are for a hexagonal washer-top lampshade measuring 7" (18cm) across the top x 12" (30.5cm) across the bottom x 8" (20.5cm) high. Adjust according to the height of your shade.

materials

antique or new maps

7" x 12" x 8" (18cm x 30.5cm 20.5cm) galvanized hexagonal uno or washer-top frame

½ yd (46cm) pressure-sensitive styrene

1½ yd (1.4m) ⅜"- (9mm-) wide cotton/rayon grosgrain ribbon

2 yd (1.8m) ⅝"- (16mm-) wide cotton/rayon grosgrain ribbon

2 yd (1.8m) decorative trim for the top and bottom of the shade

basic lampshade-making supplies (page 14)

Antique Map Shade

I don't support tearing maps out of rare books—or any books for that matter—but this one had come completely unglued, and the pages just screamed lampshade! Don't worry if the map you choose is ripped or worn; you can work around the imperfections easily, or embrace them, as I do. If you can't find a vintage map, dip a new one in brewed black tea to achieve a similar look. Distress the paper a bit first to make it look authentic. If the vintage aesthetic doesn't work in your home, consider making a lampshade out of a clean, new map. It can be a terrific way to preserve memories. Perhaps you have a nautical map that shows your favorite mooring sites, or a ski trail map of your favorite slope, or even a topographical map of your last big hike—you can really get creative with this project. For my shade, I reduced the horizontal maps by 10 percent and the vertical ones by 20 percent. Reduce according to your frame size.

step 1

steps 3–4

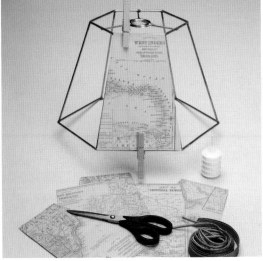

step 5

step 9

[1] On a clean work surface, spread out the maps so that you can pinpoint the places on them that you want to incorporate onto the shade. Make copies of the maps using the best color photocopier or printer available to you. If you're copying black and white images, it is still best to use a color printer; you will be much happier with the depth of the color variations.

[2] To make a template for the panels, cut out a piece of styrene just slightly bigger than a panel on the frame. Clip it to the top and bottom of the frame with clothespins. Using an ultra-thin permanent marker, trace along the outside of the panel onto the styrene. Cut out the panel.

[3] Working with one copy at a time, hold the shade frame over the copy to see what will be included in the panel. Shift the placement as desired. Place the template onto the map and trace around it with the permanent marker. Cut out. Repeat with the remaining copies.

[4] Laminate the copies to the styrene, taking care to smooth it gently with your hands to prevent bubbles or wrinkles. Cut out.

[5] Place panels in a pile in the order that you want to arrange them on the shade. Follow steps 9–12 of the Basic Lampshade-Making Technique, pages 16–17.

[6] Carefully remove the ribbon and clothespins from the shade when it is dry; it is very easy to rip the paper.

[7] Cut six strips of ⅜"- (9mm-) wide grosgrain to the length of the vertical ribs. Apply several beads of glue to a grosgrain strip and press onto a rib with your fingers to seal firmly. Remove any excess glue with your fingertip. Repeat with the remaining strips.

[8] To add grosgrain around the top and bottom of the shade, follow steps 18–20 of the Basic Lampshade-Making Technique, page 18. The top and bottom lengths of ribbon should be cut 1" (2.5cm) longer than the circumference of the top and bottom of the shade.

[9] To adhere the decorative trim to the top and bottom of the shade, glue a few inches of it at a time over the grosgrain, securing with clothespins as you go. Remove the clothespins as the glue sets to avoid indentations in the trim.

UNO-TOP SHADES

The Antique Map Shade shown features an uno-top shade. Unlike a washer-top shade, which attaches to a harp, and a clip shade, which attaches directly to the lightbulb, an uno-top shade threads onto the socket itself. Often used with iron floor or bridge lamps, uno-top shades provide soft, yet directed task lighting at just the right intensity. (I love to bask under mine when reading and knitting.) Unfortunately, pre-made uno shades can be difficult to find in retail shops—a good reason to make your own! If the lamp you're fitting was not designed for an uno-top shade, you can adapt the shade to fit a harp by using an uno adapter, which fits snugly into the uno opening.

sheet music shade

materials

6 sheets favorite antique or new sheet music

7" x 12" x 8" (18cm x 30.5cm x 20.5cm) hexagonal washer frame

½ yd (46cm) pressure-sensitive styrene

1½ yd (1.4m) ⅜"- (9mm-) wide cotton/rayon grosgrain ribbon

2 yd (1.8m) ⅝"- (16mm-) wide cotton/rayon grosgrain ribbon

2 yd (1.8m) ½"- (13mm-) wide decorative trim

basic lampshade-making supplies (page 14)

Once you've learned how to make lampshades using paper, instead of fabric, you'll have even more opportunities to create just the right shade for any room. This variation would be the perfect accessory for the piano or a music room.

Sheet music shades compel one to take a closer look. I have made these shades with both scores and album covers to great effect. This shade features sheet music dating back to the late 1800s; I always use those that are out of copyright—published before 1923. This finished shade is shown on a lamp I made with scrap metal tubing and scrap cast iron. It's good and sturdy and a nice height for a music room.

To make this shade, follow the instructions for the Antique Map Shade, page 33, but be sure to keep the following in mind:

- When making photocopies of the sheet music, reduce each sheet of music to fit the panels, about 8" (20.5cm) high. Alternatively, copy the sheets at full size and crop them to fit the panels. Make one copy of each sheet of music.

- Choose a decorative trim to enhance the shade based on colors from the sheet music.

finished measurements

All materials are for hexagonal clip shade measuring 5" (12.5cm) across the top x 10" (25.5cm) across the bottom x 7" (18cm) high. Adjust according to the size of your shade.

materials

twelve 4" x 6" (10cm x 15cm) photos in color or black and white, or 6 if enlarging to use one photo per panel

5" x 10" x 7" (12.5cm x 25.5cm x 18cm) hexagonal clip frame

½ yd (46cm) pressure-sensitive styrene

1½ yd (1.4m) ⅜"- (9mm-) wide cotton/rayon grosgrain ribbon, cut into six 7" (18cm) strips

1½ yd (1.4m) each ⅝"- (16mm) wide cotton/rayon grosgrain ribbon in 2 different colors

3 sheets 8½" x 11" (21.5cm x 28cm) white 20-lb copy paper

masking tape

basic lampshade-making supplies (page 14)

Heirloom Photo Shade

This might just be the most cherished gift you could give someone: an original work of art, photo album, instant heirloom, and decorative shade all in one. I love to use old family photos and pictures of beloved pets; but travel images and nature photos work nicely, too. I have made these shades for retirement and wedding gifts as well as for grandparents in nursing homes, an especially poignant way for an elderly person to show off family!

[1] Layout the photos as desired on each sheet of copy paper. To make a 12 photo shade that will display 2 photos per panel, position wider photos at the bottom. Tape the photos to the paper so that there is no space between the top and bottom photo.

[2] Make copies of the photos, using the best laser color photocopier or printer available to you. If copying black and white images, it is still best to use a color printer; you will be much happier with the depth of the color variations.

steps 1–2   steps 3–4   step 9

[3] Place the styrene on a clean work surface. Lay the shade frame on its side and roughly trace around it with an ultra-thin permanent marker, adding ½" (13mm) on all sides. Using the marker lines as your guide, cut out the panel. Mark the template to fit the shade panel by clipping it to the shade frame and tracing around it with the marker. Trim the excess along the line.

[4] Working with one photocopy at a time, place the template onto it and trace around it with the permanent marker. Cut out. Repeat with the remaining photocopies.

[5] Laminate the copies to the styrene, taking care to smooth it gently with your hands to prevent bubbles or wrinkles from forming. Cut out.

[6] Place the panels in a pile in the order in which you want to arrange them on the shade. Follow steps 9–12 of the Basic Lampshade-Making Technique, pages 16–17.

[7] Carefully remove the ribbon and clothespins from the shade when it is dry; it is very easy to rip the paper.

[8] Cut six strips of ⅜"- (9mm-) wide grosgrain to the length of the vertical ribs. Apply several beads of glue to a grosgrain strip and press the grosgrain onto a rib with your fingers to seal firmly. Remove any excess glue with your fingertip. Repeat with the remaining strips.

[9] To add grosgrain around the top and bottom of the shade, follow steps 18–20 in the Basic Lampshade-Making Technique, page 18. The top and bottom lengths of grosgrain ribbon should be cut 1" (2.5cm) longer than the circumference of the top and bottom of the shade. If using 2 different colors of self-trim to create a layered trim effect, affix the second color in the same manner on top of the first one so that about ⅛" (3mm) of the first trim is showing.

TIP: My motto when it comes to photo shades is "Smaller is better." Not only do larger ones present aesthetic problems, but they also introduce practical challenges: It is much more difficult to laminate large sheets of paper without creating bubbles and wrinkles.

variation

vintage
postcard shade

materials

twelve 6" x 4" (15cm x 10cm) vintage or new postcards

5" x 10" x 7" (12.5cm x 25.5cm x 18cm) hexagonal clip shade frame

½ yd (46cm) pressure-sensitive styrene

1 yd (91cm) ⅜"- (9mm-) wide cotton/rayon grosgrain ribbon

1½ yd (1.4m) ⅝"- (16mm-) wide cotton/rayon grosgrain ribbon

1½ yd (1.4m) ⅛"- (3mm-) wide cotton/rayon grosgrain ribbon or soutache in contrasting color

3 sheets 8½" x 11" (21.5cm x 28cm) white 20-lb copy paper

masking tape

basic lampshade-making supplies (page 14)

Collecting postcards is another of my passions. I like to find cards that are stained, a little rough around the edges and with writing on the front because it lends an air of authenticity to them. And because they're not in perfect shape, they're usually a little less expensive. Of course, you can make these with postcards you collect from your travels as well.

To make this shade, follow the instructions for the Heirloom Photo Shade, page 38, but be sure to keep the following in mind:

- For this project, horizontal postcards work best.

- If the postcards you've chosen have any text on them, tape them to the copy paper in step 1 so that the words fall in the middle of the shade. For example, if a card contains text on the bottom, set the card on the top of the page so that the writing will show in the middle. Likewise, if a card features text on the top, position it on the bottom of the page so the type will read in the middle.

- Don't be shy about displaying the handwritten messages on the backs of the postcards.

finished measurements

All materials are for an empire shade measuring 5" (12.5cm) across the top x 9" (23cm) across the bottom x 7" (18cm) high. Adjust according to the size of your shade.

materials

one 11" x 13" (28cm x 33cm) sheet heavyweight paper, such as watercolor or lampshade paper

5" (12.5cm) clip top

9" (23cm) bottom wire

1½ yd (1.4m) ⅝"- (16mm-) wide cotton/rayon grosgrain ribbon for the top and bottom of the shade, plus additional for the trim, if desired (I used mini pom-poms for the bottom and decorative trims for the top.)

Pastels, crayons, rubber stamps, buttons, sequins, felt flowers,

stickers and other small decorative items found at craft stores

hole punch, optional, to make a border along the bottom

glue gun, optional, if quick glue isn't strong enough to handle heavy buttons, sequins, and so on

lampshade arc template (Template, page 153)

basic lampshade-making supplies (page 14)

Kid's Hand-Colored Shade

I know the dilemma: So much of your child's artwork and so little space to hang it. Here's a solution that will make him or her puff up with pride every time you turn on the light—and will give you a new way to display your budding Picasso's talents. This project is great to have on hand for an inclement Saturday or as a school project when it's your turn to play art teacher.

Arc patterns of all sizes are available in lampshade supply catalogs. Arc patterns are inexpensive and far easier to buy than draw by hand! It took me many years before I trusted myself to draw my own lampshade arcs. This shade is a nice size, and the slant is not so steep that it is difficult for an adult to put together—the steeper the slant, the more challenging it is to make. Finally, this shade clips onto a lightbulb, making it easy to find a lamp base to fit it.

[1] Photocopy the template from page 153 twice at 142%. Cut out the templates and tape them together to make 1 long curved arc. Trace the lampshade arc onto the heavyweight paper. Cut out.

[2] Decorate the paper, first coloring it entirely so that as little white as possible shows. Next use the quick glue to adhere any buttons, sequins, felt flowers, or other chosen decorations. Advise children that ½" (13mm) all around the top and bottom of the shade will be covered by trims and glue; suggest they do not put their favorite designs there. If using the hole punch to make borders, be sure the holes are at least ½" (13mm) from the edges.

[3] With the wrong side up, run a bead of glue along the top edge of the heavyweight paper. Wrap the shade around the clip top, glue-side to frame. Fasten with clothespins as you work around the clip top. The sides of the paper will overlap in the back. Be sure the wire is set along the very edge of the arc, or the shade will be off-center.

[4] Turn the shade upside down to glue the bottom wire in place. Set the bottom wire in place at the edge of the bottom of the shade, and secure with clothespins. Check both the top and bottom wires to be sure they're flush against the edges of the arc.

[5] To glue the bottom wire in place, run a bead of glue inside the shade where the wire and paper meet. Work around the rim until you reach the back where the lampshade paper overlaps. Run a bead of glue down the inside of the back overlap and hand-press to secure. Let it dry for 20 minutes. Use the time to help children choose trims.

[6] Trim any excess paper off the top and bottom with scissors. Cut the grosgrain into 2 lengths, each 1" (2.5cm) longer than the top and bottom circumferences of the shade. Add grosgrain trim to the top and bottom of the shade, following steps 18–20 in the Basic Lampshade-Making Technique, page 18.

[7] If you're using additional trim, add glue a few inches at a time and secure the trim with clothespins.

elements of the shade

step 2

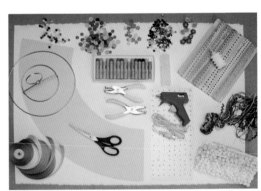

step 3

step 7

nighty-night
night-light

materials

6"- (15cm-) square piece of fabric

night-light kit

1 yd (91cm) ⅝"- (15.9mm-) wide cotton/rayon grosgrain ribbon, cut into two 4" (10cm) lengths for the side, one 5" (12.5cm) length for the top, and one 6" (15cm) length for the bottom

3" (7.5cm) length scrapbooking trim or other decorative trim

6" (15cm) length pom-pom fringe or other trim

basic lampshade-making supplies (page 14)

This kit-based lampshade is my go-to project for the tween crowd. I've taught this project at local public schools as a visiting artist and have found that it is most appropriate for eleven- to thirteen-year-olds.

A basic night-light kit (available at craft and lampshade stores or online (Resources, page 156) includes the half-round-shaped frame, the lightbulb and switch, and the styrene—you supply the fabric and a few basic lampshade-making tools.

- Remove the paper backing from the styrene and use the paper as a template. Place it on the fabric as desired. Cut out the fabric and laminate it to the styrene included in the night-light kit. Press with your hands to remove any creases or bubbles. Trim the panel of excess fabric.

- Run a bead of glue on the side of the frame and attach a 4" (10cm) strip of grosgrain lengthwise, allowing half the width to hang off the back of the shade. Add two rows of glue to the back of this overhang and wrap it around the wire. Repeat for the other side and attach the grosgrain to the top and bottom in the same manner.

- Add the decorative trim on top of the grosgrain.

intermediate shades

finished measurements

All materials are for a square frame measuring 7" (18cm) across the top x 13" (33cm) across the bottom x 12" (30.5cm) high. Adjust according to the size of your shade.

materials:

2 vintage paper flour sacks, a little larger than supermarket paper bags

7" x 13" x 12" (18cm x 33cm x 30.5cm) square frame

1 yd (91cm) pressure-sensitive styrene

4 yd (3.7m) ⅝"- (16mm-) wide cotton/rayon grosgrain ribbon

2½ yd (2.3m) ½"- (13mm-) wide decorative trim

spray adhesive

basic lampshade-making supplies (page 14)

Vintage Flour Sack Shade

It was one of those moments of Sunday antiquing glee when I spotted these old paper flour sacks at my friend Sally's antique shop. I found a pair of sacks with the same design—perfect for making this shade! The paper flour sacks are a good example of how you can turn practically any paper ephemera into a shade. In this case, the bags defined the shape of the shade. They are clearly suited to a square shade, one in which the twin graphics could go on the front and back and the plain sacks on either side. If you can't find paper sacks, use other vintage ephemera—old posters and packaging make great shades.

Using spray adhesive ensures that the sack laminates properly. Be sure to use it in a well-ventilated space. I always lay down layers of newspaper on my work surface when I am using spray adhesive. I remove a layer of paper when it is covered in adhesive so that I'm always working on a clean surface. Once finished, clean the nozzle so that it does not clog.

[1] On a clean work surface, set the frame on its side over the graphics on the bag. Using a marker, trace around the outside of the frame on the part of the bag you want to use for the shade. Flip the shade onto the remaining 3 sides and trace. Cut out the 4 panels.

[2] In a well-ventilated space and on a work surface covered with newspapers, place the panels wrong side up. Working with one panel at a time, spray with a heavy coat of adhesive (the paper really soaks it up) and set onto the styrene, taking care to avoid drips. Smooth with your hand to press out any bubbles.

[3] Follow the instructions in step 9–13 of the Basic Lampshade-Making Technique, pages 16–17.

[4] Carefully remove the ribbon and clothespins from the shade when it is dry; it is very easy to rip the paper.

[5] Cut four 12" (30.5cm) strips of ⅝"-(16mm-) wide grosgrain. Working with one strip of grosgrain at a time, run several beads of glue onto it and affix it to a vertical rib of the shade. Repeat with remaining strips of grosgrain.

[6] Add the grosgrain around the top and bottom of the shade, followed by the self-trim, following steps 18–21 of the Basic Lampshade-Making Technique, page 18.

TIPS: For the trim color, use a strong color from the bag or ephemera—it will really help pull the shade's design together. I could have stopped at the grosgrain, but I think the decorative flower trim is a snappy addition.

• Do a practice run with the spray adhesive by spraying it on scrap paper to see how it responds. In some cases, it makes unsightly splotches if it doesn't come out of the spray nozzle evenly.

elements of the shade

step 1

step 6

Antique French Ticking Chandelier Shade

finished measurements

All materials are for a square bell candle-clip frame measuring 2" (5cm) across the top x 4" (10cm) across the bottom x 4" (10cm) high. Adjust according to the size of your shade.

materials

¼ yd (23cm) antique or new French ticking

2" x 4" x 4" (5cm x 10cm x 10cm) square bell frame with candle clip

¼ yd (23cm) pressure-sensitive styrene

1 yd (91cm) ⅝"- (16mm-) wide cotton/rayon grosgrain ribbon

1 yd (91cm) pressure-sensitive cloth tape (bias-backer tape)

basic lampshade-making supplies (page 14)

Antique French Ticking Chandelier Shade

Vintage cotton ticking is the fabric that was once ubiquitous on mattresses and pillowcases. Indeed, you may find dealers with stacks of the stuff that has been torn from mattresses and (mostly) defeathered. Antique ticking has become very popular in the past decade or so—decorators find ways to use it in even the most formal interiors, whether in reds, blues, yellows, khaki, creams, and the less-common damask. Be sure you have a good look at the textile before purchasing it to ensure that it is free of stains, holes, and other discolorations that will instantly show when you shine a light through it. Stay away from damask ticking; the patterns are pretty but they don't show up very well when lit.

Self-trims are a natural choice when using ticking fabrics. Simply run the cloth tape along a stripe for a self-trim, or set it on the bias for a striped self-trim.

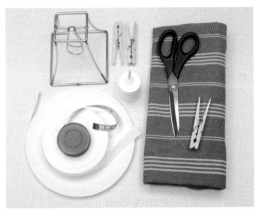

elements of the shade

steps 2–5

[1] Follow steps 1–4 of the Basic Lampshade-Making Technique, page 14, to cut out the styrene panels.

[2] With the fabric wrong side up, iron it so that it is perfectly crisp and wrinkle free. Ironing the fabric well helps to ensure accuracy when you are ready to laminate your panels.

[3] Turn the fabric right side up and place it on a clean work surface. Study the possibilities for placing the design on your shade. If you are using a ticking with variegated stripes, alternate the sets of stripes on the panels of your shade to give it a balanced look.

[4] Turn the fabric over so that it is wrong side up. When laminating any striped fabric, it is critical to ensure that the stripes are perfectly straight. If they are the least bit crooked, it will be instantly noticeable. My method is to line up the bottom edge of the styrene panels so that the stripes on the ironed fabric are perpendicular to the edge. Working with one panel at a time, remove the paper backing from the styrene and place the styrene on the back of the fabric as desired. Press with your hand to adhere. As with other styrene projects, do *not* iron, as the styrene will melt. Flip the fabric over and look at it from the front to make sure your design is where you intended it to be. Constantly check to make sure the fabric is straight as you cut out the panel.

step 6

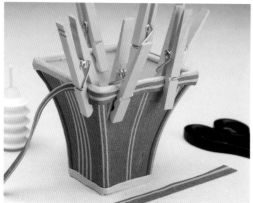

applying the self-trim

Lampshade Lady favorites

[5] Repeat with the remaining panels of styrene and fabric.

[6] Follow steps 9–21 of the Basic Lampshade-Making Technique, pages 16–18.

TIP: Remember to use low-wattage bulbs with these small shades. Too high a wattage will melt the styrene.

IF THE SHADE FITS . . .

The square bell candle-clip shade used here fits nicely on chandeliers as well as wall sconces. Other shades perfect for them include hexagonal, hexagonal bell, scallop, square, and empire shapes. The very old wall sconce I used is wired for a regular bulb, but I was able to use a lightbulb with a candle top but a regular-size screw-in bottom. You just have to experiment!

Funky Floral Feed Sack Shade

finished measurements

All materials are for a hexagonal bell clip shade measuring 5" (12.5cm) across the top x 8" (20.5cm) across the bottom x 6" (15cm) high. Adjust according to the size of your shade.

materials

2 or 3 different feed sacks or cotton floral fabrics

5" x 8" x 6" (12.5cm x 20.5cm x 15cm) hexagonal bell clip frame

½ yd (46cm) pressure-sensitive styrene

1½ yd (1.4m) ⅝"- (16mm-) wide cotton/rayon grosgrain ribbon

2½ yd (2.3m) ¼"- or ⁵⁄₁₆"- (6mm- or 8mm-) wide pressure-sensitive cloth tape (bias-trim backer), cut into six 6" (15cm) lengths

basic lampshade-making supplies (page 14)

Funky Floral Feed Sack Shade

Anyone who is old enough to remember the television show *The Waltons* knows what a feed sack is but may not know that the dresses Olivia, Mary Ellen, Erin, and Elizabeth wore were made from the sacks that Pa brought home from the general store. Once emptied of the sugar, flour, chicken feed, or rice, the fabric bags, about one full yard (91cm), were ideal for reuse. In some cases, the sacks became instant aprons or tea towels with the removal of a single string—no sewing necessary. It took about three sacks to make a woman's dress—that's a lot of grain to go through!

Patterned sacks began appearing in the early 1940s. Prior to that, the bulk of feed sacks carried advertising for the mills and companies from which the consumables inside came. In some cases, housewives would wash them until the ink came off and then stitch them into dresses. An enterprising stockholder in a grain company in Tennessee came up with the ingenious idea of printing florals on feed sacks, making them all the more appealing to housewives. They were made in three different versions of cotton, from coarse to fine cotton muslin. It is thought that at one point in the 1940s more than 3 million Americans were wearing dresses crafted from feed sacks. With the advent of plastic bags, the sacks eventually disappeared.

Even so, turning them into shades is a great—and lasting—way to enjoy them. I prefer to use a mix of different florals in a single shade, but there are no rules. If you find only one, or simply prefer a continuous pattern, by all means cut your shade panels from a single sack.

[1] Cut out the lampshade panels following steps 1–4 of the Basic Lampshade-Making Technique, page 14.

[2] With the fabric wrong side up, iron it so that it is wrinkle free. Turn the fabric right side up and place it on a clean work surface. Study it carefully, making note of any fabric pulls, stains, or holes. You will want to avoid these when adhering the styrene to the fabric.

elements of the shade

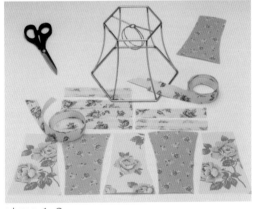

steps 1–3

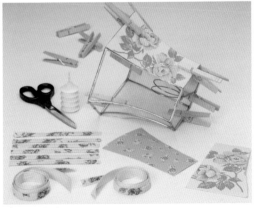

steps 4–6

step 7

[3] Turn the fabric over so that it is wrong side up. Be sure that the pattern on the fabric—in this case, the floral—is going in the right direction; you don't want some of the panels showing the flowers with the blooms pointing toward the bottom of the shade and others going the right way, with the blooms pointing toward the top. Follow steps 7–8 of the Basic Lampshade-Making Technique, page 15, to adhere the styrene to the fabric.

[4] Place the frame on a work surface. Find the solder mark on the bottom rim of the frame. Start here when recutting to fit your first fabric-covered panel. You may need to work and rework the panel several times, depending on the shade. Place the panel on the frame and secure with clothespins. If you are using a symmetrical frame, such as a square or a drum, be sure that the fabric panel is positioned properly—you don't want the design to be upside down! Trim the styrene so that it just meets the frame on all sides. Remove it from the frame and mark it with a very tiny number 1 on the back at the bottom. (Don't make the number large, or it will show through your shade when it's lit; the trim will cover a tiny mark.)

[5] Working clockwise around the frame, refit and recut each panel, securing it with clothespins to the frame and marking it with a number as you go.

[6] Beginning with the first panel on the soldered side of the frame, run a very light bead of glue around this section of the frame, at the top, bottom, and sides. Set the panel in place and clip with a clothespin on the top and bottom. Continue affixing the panels to the frame in this fashion, working clockwise and in order of the numbered panels.

[7] Finish the shade following steps 12–21 of the Basic Lampshade-Making Technique, pages 17–18.

TIPS: Most textile dealers will have washed their feed sacks before putting them out for sale. Be sure that this is the case, or that you wash the fabric before storing it or turning it into a lampshade. It should be free of mold and mildew and any foodstuffs (such as grain) that might attract rodents. Be sure to look over the textile thoroughly, keeping an eye out for holes that you won't be able to work around.

· Quilt shops often stock reproduction feed sack fabrics, which could be handy for matching with a vintage sack.

mama's pretty apron shade

materials

2 vintage aprons or about ¼ yd (23cm) vintage fabric

5" x 8" x 6" (12.5cm x 20.5cm x 15cm) hexagonal bell frame

½ yard (46cm) pressure-sensitive styrene

1½ yd (1.4m) ⅝"- (16mm-) wide cotton/rayon grosgrain ribbon

1 yd (91cm) ⁵⁄₁₆"- (8mm-) wide pressure-sensitive cloth tape (bias-trim backer)

¾ yd (69cm) rickrack for the top of the shade

1 yd (91cm) ½"- (13mm-) wide jacquard trim or other decorative trim for the bottom of the shade

basic lampshade-making supplies (page 14)

Vintage aprons may be too cutesy to wear while cooking dinner these days, but they are ideal for turning into lampshades. I have a treasure trove of them, which made it really hard to choose just one to demonstrate here! Nevertheless, this charming rosy print caught my eye quickly enough. For the ribs, I used a fabric from a different apron and then chose two different trims for the top and bottom of the shade.

To make this shade, follow the instructions for the Funky Floral Feed Sack Shade, page 55, but be sure to keep the following in mind:

- Once you've ironed the apron, look over the fabric very carefully, making a note of tears, pulls, and especially stains. It is rare to find a pristine vintage apron, so you'll want to work around areas that are stained or permanently soiled. If they do end up on one of your panels, the unsightly spots will most certainly show when the light is turned on. Also, note that if you've removed pockets from the apron, the fabric underneath will likely be brighter than the rest of the apron.

finished measurements

All materials are for a rectangular washer-top shade measuring 9" x 7" (23cm x 18cm) across the top, 14" x 10" (35.5cm x 25.5cm) across the bottom x 10" (25.5cm) high. Adjust according to the size of your shade.

materials

1 yd (91cm) cotton fabric with large floral print

9" x 7" (23cm x 18cm) x 14" x 10" (35.5cm x 25.5cm) x 10" (25.5cm) rectangular washer-top shade frame

1 yd (91cm) pressure-sensitive styrene

2½ yd (2.3m) ⅝"- (16mm-) wide cotton/rayon grosgrain ribbon for the top and bottom of the shade

1½ yd (1.4m) ¼"- or ⁵⁄₁₆"- (6mm- or 8mm-) wide pressure-sensitive cloth tape (bias-trim backer)

2½ yd (2.3m) trim for the top and bottom of the shade

basic lampshade-making supplies (page 14)

Cool Cottage Flowers Shade

This is a nice, big shade that can really make a statement when you choose a gregarious floral print. Depending on the interior, however, it can be just as striking in a solid neutral because the shape of the shade itself is so graphic. It has real presence set on a squat base. I just love this particular print, especially in a summer house—you can almost smell the blooms! The top and bottom trim is polka-dot scrapbooking ribbon, available at any craft store.

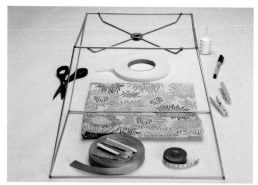
elements of the shade

steps 1–5

step 6

[1] Place the styrene on a clean work surface. Lay the shade frame on its larger side and roughly trace around it with an ultra-thin permanent marker. Move the frame to a clean part of the styrene, turn it onto its smaller side, and roughly trace around it with the permanent marker. Using the marker lines as your guide, cut out the 2 panels, adding about ½" (13mm) on all sides.

[2] Using clothespins, clip the larger panel to the larger side of the frame at the top and bottom. Using the permanent marker, mark the styrene along the exterior of the frame panel. This will give you a more precise measure of the panel. Cut out. Repeat with the smaller panel.

[3] Using the 2 panels as your templates, cut out one more of each. Set aside.

[4] Prepare a hot iron. Place the fabric wrong side up on the ironing board. Iron until the fabric is smooth and creaseless. You may need to use starch, depending on the fabric.

[5] With the fabric wrong side up, remove the paper backing from the styrene and adhere to the fabric where desired, pressing with your hand to seal the lamination. Repeat with the remaining panels and fabric.

[6] Follow steps 9–21 of the Basic Lampshade-Making Technique, pages 16–18. Use a trim of your choice around the top and bottom of the shade.

ALL ABLOOM

Fabrics have blossomed in the past few years, and the small calico prints of yesteryear have been replaced by big, exuberant floral patterns. Many young textile designers are bringing new life to traditional cottons. These contemporary fabrics are great on lampshades. Use them on drums, squares, rectangles, or whatever your favorite shape. As you work with these cottons, be aware that their smooth surface can make lamination more difficult. With this type of fabric, keep a bottle of spray adhesive handy to tack down the fabric to the styrene panels, if necessary.

Country Candlewicking Shade

finished measurements

All materials are for a square bell shade measuring 4" (10cm) across the top x 7" (18cm) across the bottom x 7" (18cm) high. Adjust according to the size of your shade.

materials

½ yd (46cm) vintage candlewicking from a bedspread or dresser scarf, or scavenged scraps or small pieces

4" x 7" x 7" (10cm x 18cm x 18cm) square bell shade frame

½ yd (46cm) pressure-sensitive styrene

1½ yd (1.3m) ⅝"- (16mm-) wide cotton/rayon grosgrain ribbon

1 yd (91cm) ¼"- or ⁵⁄₁₆"- (6mm- or 8mm-) wide pressure-sensitive cloth tape (bias-trim backer)

1½ yd (1.3m) decorative trim for the top and bottom of the shade (choose 2 different trims if desired)

basic lampshade-making supplies (page 14)

Country Candle-wicking Shade

Candlewicking is a type of embroidery in which designs are stitched on fabric with the heavy cotton thread used to make candle wicks. Knots known as colonial stitches are most commonly used; these are made with six strands of the cotton thread. The result is an embroidery so thick that it casts shadows on the muslin typically used for the foundation. While I like to be playful with vertical self-trims, in this case I prefer to use either a length of plain muslin or, even better, a length of candlewicking, if you have it. On the top and bottom, I've used two different contrasting trims in a related theme: leaves and flowers.

Candlewicking is found on bedspreads, tablecloths, and table runners. The quality varies as wildly as the makers do. I always look for damaged or stained candlewicking if I'm going to cut it up for a shade; a perfect piece is too valuable, both sentimentally and monetarily, to touch with scissors. Although candlewicking may have a connotation of "ye olde," it is anything but when applied like this.

elements of the shade

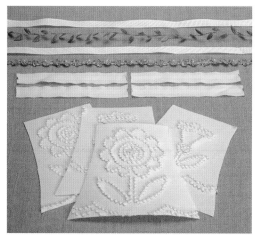

steps 1–4

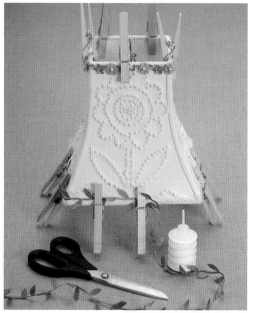

step 5

[1] Cut 4 panels of styrene to fit your square bell shade frame according to steps 1–4 of the Basic Lampshade-Making Technique, page 14.

[2] With the fabric wrong side up, iron it so that it is wrinkle free. Trim away any loose threads on the back of the candlewicking fabric. In addition, cut the long thread carries, the stretches of thread that are carried along the back between stitched designs. If left untrimmed, these threads will show through the shade once the light is turned on. Do this carefully—you don't want to snip through the fabric!

[3] Place the fabric on a clean work surface. Continue assembling the shade, following steps 6–12 of the Basic Lampshade-Making Technique, pages 15–17.

[4] Cut the grosgrain ribbon and make the self-trim, following steps 13–15 of the Basic Lampshade-Making Technique, page 17. For the vertical self-trim, use the remaining candlewicking fabric.

[5] Complete the shade by following steps 16–21 of the Basic Lampshade-Making Technique, pages 17–18.

finished measurements

All materials are for a square bell shade measuring 4" (10cm) across the top x 7" (18cm) across the bottom x 7" (18cm) high. Adjust according to the size of your shade.

materials

½ yd (46cm) vintage or new Marimekko fabric

4" x 7" x 7" (10cm x 18cm x 18cm) square bell shade frame

¼ yd (23cm) pressure-sensitive styrene

1½ yd (1.4m) ⅝"- (16mm-) wide cotton/rayon grosgrain ribbon

2¼ yd (2m) ¼"- or ⁵⁄₁₆"- (6mm- or 8mm-) pressure-sensitive cloth tape (bias-trim backer)

basic lampshade-making supplies (page 14)

My Favorite Marimekko Shade

Leave it to Jackie Kennedy to turn Americans on to Scandinavian style, namely Marimekko, the Finnish design company known for their bright, graphic patterns designed for fashion and the home. During the '60s and '70s Marimekko was all the rage. It was a new era, ready to challenge the old styles. I spent my high school summers as a nanny for a family who lived on Boston's North Shore. On my day off each week, I would make a beeline for the Marimekko shop on Newbury Street. There was little I could afford in there on my nanny's salary, but I always managed to come away with a bag from the scraps bin. Once a rag picker, always a rag picker! By the end of the summer I had enough pieces for a quilt and a mini skirt, and I was so blindly proud of my skirt that I wore it to a family funeral! I am particularly fond of this flower Marimekko pattern, especially on a bell-shaped shade. Some of the company's bolder, larger designs are great for large drum shades.

[1] Cut 4 panels of styrene to fit your square bell shade frame according to steps 1–4 of the Basic Lampshade-Making Technique, page 14.

[2] With the fabric wrong side up, iron it so that it is wrinkle free. Turn the fabric right side up and place it on a clean work surface. Study the possibilities for placing the design on your shade.

[3] Turn the fabric over so that it is wrong side up. If it has a pattern with a distinct top and bottom, be sure to position the fabric on the work surface so that you are placing the styrene panels in the proper direction. Working with one panel at a time, follow steps 7–12 of the Basic Lampshade-Making Technique, pages 15–17, to create the panels and attach them to the frame.

[4] Cut the grosgrain ribbon and make the self-trim, following steps 13–15 of the Basic Lampshade-Making Technique, page 17. If your fabric has a stripe or great colors, incorporate the fabric design into the shade trim. When applying the glue for the self-trims, be generous, as the fabric tends to soak it up.

[5] Finish assembly of the shade, following steps 16–21 of the Basic Lampshade-Making Technique, pages 17–18. As you apply the self-trim to the shade, keep in mind that working around the corners can be a little tricky. Give the trim a gentle tug to help it around the corners.

elements of the shade

steps 1–3

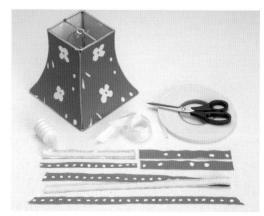

steps 4–5

NOTE: To accompany my favorite Marimekko fabric, I just had to choose my favorite lamp, handcrafted by my friend Janno Gay. Her shop in Dorset, Vermont, fairly bursts with her creative pottery. In my humble opinion, Janno has designed the lamp of the century!

Visit Janno at her shop, Flower Brook Pottery, Route 30 and Dorset Hollow Road, or online at www.flowerbrookpottery.com. Or just call her up at 802–867–2409. You can tell her The Lampshade Lady sent you.

nursery rhyme embroidery shade

materials

1 vintage embroidery, sized appropriately for shade

½ yd (46cm) popcorn chenille or other cotton fabric

4" x 7" x 7" (10cm x 18cm x 18cm) square bell clip shade frame, preferably galvanized

½ yd (46cm) pressure-sensitive styrene

1½ yd (1.3m) ⅝"- (16mm-) wide cotton/rayon grosgrain ribbon

1 yd (91cm) ¼" to ½"- (6mm–13mm-) wide trim for vertical ribs

1½ yd (1.4m) ½"- (13mm-) wide trim for the top and bottom of the shade

basic lampshade-making supplies (page 14)

This darling shade makes a wonderful baby gift—amid all the onesies, rattles, and baby gear, it will stand out for sure. Vintage embroideries with children's motifs were often stitched into quilts, so you might find a quilt that's been irreparably damaged but has parts that can be cut away to make a shade like this. Or, look in flea markets for quilt blocks that were never put together into a complete quilt. The popcorn chenille covering three sides of this shade is a perfect complement to the Little Bo Peep front—it reminds me of wooly sheep!

To make this shade, follow the instructions for the Country Candlewicking Shade, page 63, but be sure to keep the following in mind:

- You don't need enough embroidery to cover all four sides of this shade; I actually had plenty when I made this shade, but I chose to use it on the front of the shade only so that I could make more lampshades from the others.

- When ironing embroidery or popcorn chenille, iron with the wrong side up to prevent flattening of the stitching or chenille. Remember to trim away any loose threads from the embroidery after ironing.

finished measurements

All materials are for a square clip galvanized shade measuring 4" (10cm) across the top x 7" (18cm) across the bottom x 7" (18cm) high. Adjust according to the dimensions of your shade.

materials

vintage cloth children's book

4" x 7" x 7" (10cm x 18cm x 18cm) square galvanized clip frame

½ yd (46cm) pressure-sensitive styrene

1¾ yd (1.6m) ⅝"- (16mm-) wide cotton/rayon grosgrain ribbon

1 yd (91cm) ¼"- or ⁵⁄₁₆"- (6mm- or 8mm-) pressure-sensitive cloth tape (bias-trim backer), cut into four 7" (18cm) lengths

⅛ yd (11cm) red cotton gingham or other fabric for vertical trim

1 yd (91cm) each rickrack and pom-pom fringe or other trim for the top and bottom of the shade

seam ripper

basic lampshade-making supplies (page 14)

Child's Cloth Book Lampshade

Anyone born before, say, 1940 had an old-school cloth book. I will admit they are sometimes too adorable to cut up, but I'd rather enjoy the pages' charms all the time than stash the book somewhere and have an occasional happy memory. If you haven't socked one away in your attic, troll online auction sites or flea markets and antique shops. I let the size of the pages determine the size of this shade—all the better to get in as much of them as possible.

[1] Decide which 4 pages of the book will become the panels on your shade. If the book isn't large enough to accommodate the shade specified, downsize the frame size accordingly; or, choose a size that makes the most of the frame size.

[2] Using a seam ripper, separate the pages of the book, setting aside those you've chosen for your shade. Trim away any loose threads.

[3] Follow steps 1–20 of the Basic Lampshade-Making Technique, pages 14–18.

[4] Glue the rickrack or other trim to the top of the shade a few inches at a time, beginning at the back of the shade and positioning it so that it rises just above the rim. Overlap the ends and hold it in place with clothespins.

[5] To attach the pom-pom trim to the bottom, position it so that the straight edge is aligned with the self-trim. Hold the trim in place with clothespins, gluing in place as in the previous step. Remove the clothespins once the glue has set but before it is completely dry; you don't want the clothespins to make indentations in the trim.

elements of the shade

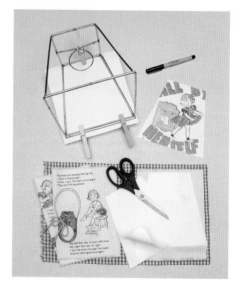

steps 2–3

attaching the pom-pom trim

steps 4–5

embroidered alphabet book shade

materials

vintage embroidered or printed cloth alphabet book

5" x 8" x 6" (12.5cm x 20.5cm x 6cm) hexagonal clip frame

¼ yd (23cm) pressure-sensitive styrene

1½ yd (1.4m) ⅝"- (16mm-) wide cotton/rayon grosgrain ribbon

1½ yd (1.4m) decorative trim for top and bottom of shade

1 yd (91cm) rickrack for vertical ribs

seam ripper

basic lampshade-making supplies (page 14)

I love the idea behind the cloth alphabet book, which was once used as a teaching tool for little ones during their formative years: They stitched the letters onto cloth and learned their ABCs at the same time. This shade is my answer to the alphabet border many parents choose when decorating the nursery.

To make this shade, follow the instructions for the Child's Cloth Book Lampshade, page 70, but be sure to keep the following in mind.

• Before laminating the embroidered book pages to the styrene, trim all the stray threads on the back of each page. Thick threads can cause lumpiness in the lamination, and can sometimes be seen through the cloth when the finished lamp is turned on.

finished measurements

All materials are for a square bell shade measuring 4½" (11.5cm) across the top x 8½" (21.5cm) across the bottom x 8" (20.5cm) high. Adjust according to the size of your shade.

materials

½ yd (46cm) Hawaiian cotton fabric

4½" x 8½" x 8" (11.5cm x 21.5cm x 20.5cm) square bell shade frame

½ yd (46cm) pressure-sensitive styrene

2 yd (1.8cm) ⅝"- (16mm-) wide cotton/rayon grosgrain ribbon

1 yd (91cm) pressure-sensitive cloth tape (bias-trim backer)

⅛ yd (11cm) contrasting fabric for vertical ribs

½ yd (46cm) ⅛"–½"- (3mm–13mm-) wide trim for the top of the shade

1 yd (91cm) beaded trim for the bottom of the shade

basic lampshade-making supplies (page 14)

Aloha Hawaiian Floral Shade

This is the shade to make if you want to go back to that little grass shack. But seriously, I wasn't in my shop more than two days after visiting friends in Kauai when I began surrounding myself with Hawaiian fabric shades. The colors and patterns are so bright and cheerful, I couldn't stop! I have found that vintage Hawaiian florals are not as easy to come by as, say, their barkcloth cousins, which would also work well on this shade. The version shown here features a new cotton fabric inspired by the vintage florals from the Aloha State. I have added a whimsical trim that sways a bit like a hula skirt.

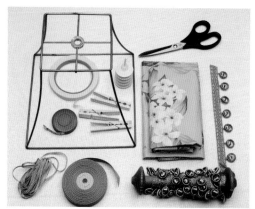

elements of the shade

steps 1–4

steps 6–7

[1] Cut out the panels for the shade, following steps 1–4 of the Basic Lampshade-Making Technique, page 14.

[2] With the fabric wrong side up, iron it so that it is wrinkle free. Turn the fabric right side up and place it on a clean work surface. Look it over and make a note of any imperfections—you will want to avoid these areas when positioning the panels on the fabric. For this shade, I chose 2 different parts of the fabric from which to make my panels so that I would have alternating patterns on the shade: a busier pattern alternating with one that has more solid background showing.

[3] Follow steps 7–12 of the Basic Lampshade-Making Technique, pages 15–17, to create the panels and fit them on the shade frame.

[4] I have used 2 different decorative trims on this shade; the vertical ribs are self-trim made from a contrasting fabric. I like to mix and match this way—it is a signature part of my work. To cut the grosgrain and make the self-trim, follow steps 13–15 of the Basic Lampshade-Making Technique, page 17.

[5] When the lampshade has dried, remove the grosgrain and clothespins. Trim away any excess styrene.

[6] Apply the self-trim and grosgrain to the vertical ribs and the top and bottom of the shade as described in steps 17–20 of the Basic Lampshade-Making Technique, pages 17–18.

[7] Apply glue to the decorative trim for the bottom of the shade and affix it to the grosgrain along the bottom of the shade. Be sure that the parts that dangle hang below the edge of the shade. Apply glue to the decorative trim for the top of the shade and affix it along the bottom of the top grosgrain, working in 3" (7.5cm) sections as you go.

Vintage French Floral Barkcloth Shade

finished measurements

All materials are for a hexagonal bell shade measuring 5" (12.5cm) across the top x 10" (25.5cm) across the bottom x 7" (18cm) high. Adjust according to the size of your shade.

materials

½ yd (46cm) vintage French barkcloth or reproduction barkcloth

5" x 10" x 7" (12.5cm x 25.5cm x 18cm) hexagonal bell frame

½ yd (46cm) pressure-sensitive styrene

1½ yd (1.4m) ⅝"- (16mm-) wide cotton/rayon grosgrain ribbon

3 yd (2.75cm) ¼"- or ⁵⁄₁₆"- (6mm- or 8mm-) pressure-sensitive cloth tape (bias-trim backer)

basic lampshade-making supplies (page 14)

Vintage French Floral Barkcloth Shade

I've long believed that people who share the same passions eventually find each other. Now that the Internet provides accessibility to just about anyone, it's easier to find fellow textile junkies. One of my favorites is Wendy, a textile dealer, known to eBay textile shoppers as Loody-Lady. We met through an eBay connection. She had just moved to Vermont from England, but it was as if I had known her all my life. She's the source for this stunning, hard-to-find, deep-red barkcloth, also known as textured cretonne, the name given to it before it made its appearance in the United States in the 1950s. If you need to give a room a touch of sophistication, this is the shade with which to do it.

TIP: In my many years of plying flea markets and estate sales, I've found that most vintage barkcloth is available in the form of drapery panels. If they are in pristine condition, they can fetch upwards of several hundred dollars. The beauty of turning them into shades is that they don't have to be perfect—you can just cut around any imperfections, such as faded spots from too many years blocking sunlight.

[1] To cut out the styrene panels, follow steps 1–4 of the Basic Lampshade-Making Technique, page 14.

[2] With the barkcloth wrong side up, iron it so that it is wrinkle free. Turn the fabric right side up and place it on a clean work surface. Study the possibilities for placing the design on your shade. Pay careful attention to any color fading that might have occurred over time.

[3] Continue assembling the lampshade following steps 7–13 of the Basic Lampshade-Making Technique, pages 15–17.

[4] To make the barkcloth self-trim, follow steps 14–15 of the Basic Lamshade-Making Technique, page 17. Barkcloth can be quite thick and difficult to fold; it might help to iron self-trims onto the cloth tape. Iron where you would fold to glue. Remember that you must smooth out any bumps and create a crisp edge.

[5] When the lampshade has dried, remove the grosgrain and clothespins. Trim away any excess styrene.

[6] Working on one vertical rib at a time, fold the self-trim in half lengthwise, wrong sides together, to create a valley. Apply glue in the valley and affix the trim

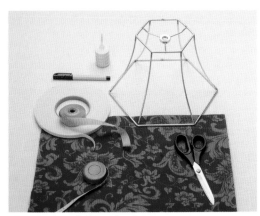

elements of the shade

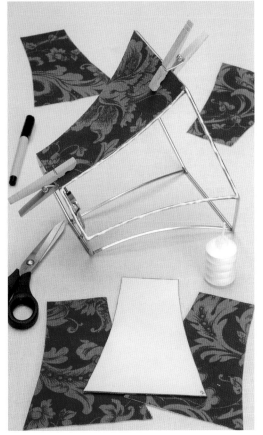

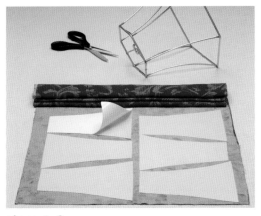

steps 1–2

step 3

to one of the ribs on the shade. When adhering the self-trims to the shade, you will need a generous amount of glue; barkcloth tends to soak it up. Repeat with the remaining pieces of trim, cutting away any excess trim, if necessary.

[7] Finish the assembly by following steps 18–21 of the Basic Lampshade-Making Technique, page 18.

step 4

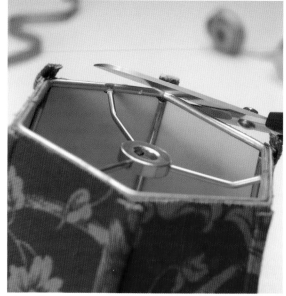

step 6

WHAT EXACTLY *IS* BARKCLOTH?

True barkcloth is exactly what you might think it is—cloth that is made from the bark of trees. The material was made by beating the moist, fibrous inner bark of trees of the Moraceae family into thin sheets. It was once common in Asia, Africa, Indonesia, and the Pacific. In home decor, the fabric that is referred to as barkcloth is not made from the bark of trees but is a thick, textured cotton that mimics the coarse surface of true barkcloth. The fabric was first made in France in the early 1900s and wasn't made in the United States until 1930. Florals predominated in barkcloth's early years, but by the mid-1940s, almost any motif imaginable made its way onto the fabric: tropicals, abstract shapes, animals, romantic scenes, you name it. By 1950, there was barely a house in the United States that did not have a bit of barkcloth in it. When more manmade fibers began to make it into the American mainstream in the 1960s, the popularity of barkcloth began to fade, save for its use in Hawaiian clothing. By 1970, it all but disappeared. But just as fashion mines the past for current looks, interior designers have begun using barkcloth in interiors they like to call retro.

variation

velvet vintage
theorem shade

materials

1½ (1.4m) yd vintage or new velvet theorem or cut velvet

5" x 10" x 7" (12.5cm x 25.5cm x 18cm) hexagonal bell frame

½ yd (46cm) pressure-sensitive styrene

1½ yd (1.4m) ⅜"- (9mm-) wide silk velvet ribbon for vertical ribs

1½ yd (1.4m) ⅝"- (16mm-) wide cotton/rayon grosgrain ribbon in a complementary color

1½ yd (1.4m) ½"- (13mm-) wide decorative velvet trim

basic lampshade-making supplies (page 14)

You've likely seen textiles like this but may not have known the technical name for them. Theorems are velvet paintings in which stencils are used to "draw" on fabric. They were all the rage at the turn of the nineteenth century in England and were part of the curriculum at women's boarding schools in colonial New England. Floral, fruit, and bird designs are among the most common.

To make this shade, follow the instructions for the Vintage French Floral Barkcloth Shade, page 77, but be sure to keep the following in mind:

- If you find only one theorem, use it for the front of the shade and use complementary fabric for the sides and back. Plan the placement of the theorem accordingly.

- In lieu of making self-trims, which would be too bulky, cut 2 lengths of the grosgrain ribbon, each 1" (2.5cm) longer than the circumference of the top and bottom of the shade, then add braided velvet decorative trim. For the vertical ribs, cut strips of silk velvet equal to the height of the shade for each rib.

finished measurements

All materials are for a hexagonal clip shade measuring 4" (10cm) across the top x 8" (20.5cm) across the bottom x 6" (15cm) high. Adjust according to the size of your shade.

materials

3–6 vintage floral cotton hankies, mixed and matched to please

4" x 8" x 6" (10cm x 20.5cm x 15cm) hexagonal clip frame

½ yd (46cm) pressure-sensitive styrene

1½ yd (1.4m) ⅝"- (16mm-) wide cotton/rayon grosgrain ribbon

1 yd (91cm) ¼"- or ⁵⁄₁₆"- (6mm- or 8mm-) wide pressure-sensitive cloth tape (bias-trim backer)

1½ yd (1.4m) self-trim made with crocheted hankie edge or the hankie fabric itself

basic lampshade-making supplies (page 14)

Granny's Floral Hankie Shade

I'm willing to bet that most of you have a hankie from your grand-mother tucked away in a bureau somewhere. There's something about the small floral squares that beg to be collected—the cotton worn to the perfect softness, the aroma of your grandma's perfume, the memory of her tucking it in her purse. I don't think I know anyone who actually uses hankies for their intended purpose anymore, which is why putting them on a lampshade seems like the perfect way to enjoy them. In every antique co-op, at most textile booths at antique fairs, and in the linens box at tag sales, there is inevitably a floral hankie. The straight floral designs are easy to come by, and so are the monogrammed varieties.

You can use up to six different hankies on this lamp. I usually cut two panels from a single hankie, which allows for mixing pretty colors in similar tones together or using similar colors or design elements, as I have here with pansy hankies.

TIP: When I'm using monogram hankies, I find that small hexagonal scallop shades showcase them beautifully. I recommend a shade sized 4" (10cm) across the top x 8" (20.5cm) across the bottom x 6" (15cm) high. The monograms are typically stitched in the corner of the hankie, so the styrene panels must be set on the bias if you want to center the monogram.

[**1**] Choose favorite hankies. You can use 6 different ones, or you can usually get 2 panels out of one hankie.

[**2**] Follow steps 1–13 of the Basic Lampshade-Making Technique, pages 14–17.

[**3**] If you're making crocheted self-trim, cut each of the four crochet edges away from the hankie, leaving ⅛" (3mm) of fabric on the edge. (You probably will not have enough material to cut the edging in one continuous piece; pieces will be spliced together to get the full length for the top and bottom trims.) Fold the extra ⅛" (3mm) of fabric back onto the back side of the crochet edging and glue together. Press with your hands to secure. Apply glue to the crocheted self-trim and set it onto the grosgrain as you would to make any self-trim, working 5" (12.5cm) at a time. If you need to add another length, simply overlap it slightly with the previous edging and glue. Where the ends meet, cut them on a diagonal so that they just overlap and adhere with glue.

[**4**] Attach your crocheted self-trim, or premade decorative trim, following steps 17–21 of the Basic Lampshade-Making Technique, pages 17–18.

elements of the shade

steps 1–2

step 3

Handsome Doggie Shade

finished measurements

All materials are for a hexagonal clip shade measuring 5" (12.5cm) across the top x 10" (25.5cm) across the bottom x 7" (18cm) high. Adjust according to the size of your shade.

materials

doggie embroidery tea towel or other decorative tea towel, new or vintage, trimmed of threads on the back side

5" x 10" x 7" (12.5cm x 25.5cm x 18cm) hexagonal clip shade frame

½ yd (46cm) pressure-sensitive styrene

1½ yd (1.4m) ⅝"- (16mm-) wide cotton/rayon grosgrain ribbon

1½ yd (1.4m) ¼"- or ⁵⁄₁₆"- (6mm- or 8mm-) wide pressure-sensitive cloth tape (bias-trim backer)

1½ yd (1.4m) ½"- (13mm-) wide decorative trim for the bottom of the shade

⅛ yd (11cm) paisley or other fabric or braid trim for vertical ribs

basic lampshade-making supplies (page 14)

Handsome Doggie Shade

Anything with a dog on it sells immediately in my shop. I found this interesting black and white tea towel in an antique mall in Quechee, Vermont. Tea towels are extremely easy to come by today; virtually every flea market or shop I've walked into has a decent stack to ponder.

I chose paisley trim for this particular shade because I thought it would soften the harshness of the black embroidery and because I love cotton paisley fabrics. The contemporary stripe used for the top and bottom trim pulls the components together to give it a crisp look. I chose the size of this shade based on the size of the towel, but in hindsight I would have chosen a slightly smaller shade (5" x 8" x 6" [12.5cm x 20.5cm x 15cm]) in the same shape so the embroidery could sit lower on the shade. Nevertheless, this shade, one of the most popular sizes in my shop, is most commonly used on floor lamps with an extended arm. It is also a good size for a desk lamp.

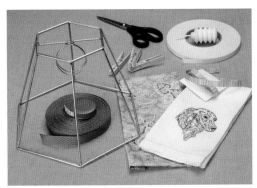

elements of the shade

steps 1–4

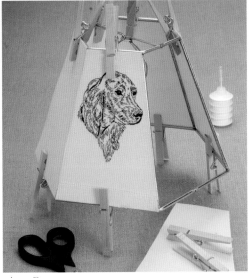

step 5

attaching the self-trim

[1] Follow steps 1–4 of the Basic Lampshade-Making Technique, page 14, to cut out the styrene panels.

[2] Iron the tea towel from the reverse. Trim any loose threads from it.

[3] Remove the paper backing from one panel of the styrene and place the styrene on the back of the tea towel, centering the design. Press with your hand to adhere. Do not iron. Cut out the panel.

[4] Repeat for the remaining 5 pieces of styrene.

[5] Follow steps 9–21 of the Basic Lampshade-Making Technique, pages 16–18.

TIP: Use the neck of the glue squeeze bottle to help spread the glue over the entire trim surface. The key is to cover it entirely with a thin coat of glue.

finished measurements

All materials are for a rectangular washer-top shade measuring 10" x 5" (25.5cm x 12.5cm) across the top, 12" x 7" (30.5cm x 18cm) across the bottom, and 8" (20.5cm) high. Adjust according to the size of your shade.

materials

½ yd (46cm) vintage or new big dotted fabric

10" x 5" (25.5cm x 12.5cm) x 12" x 7" (30.5cm x 18cm) x 8" (20.5cm) rectangular washer-top shade frame

½ yd (46cm) pressure-sensitive styrene

2½ yd (2.3m) ⅝" (15.9) wide cotton/rayon grosgrain ribbon

3 yd (2.75m) ¼"- or ⁵⁄₁₆"- (6mm- or 8mm-) wide pressure-sensitive cloth tape (bias-trim backer)

¹⁄₁₆ yd (6cm) Susan Sargent Linen Dot fabric by Robert Allen (Resources, page 156), for self-trim

16 glass beads

16 flat buttons

2¼ yd (2m) rickrack

needle and gold thread

spray adhesive

basic lampshade-making supplies (page 14)

Polka Dot Shade

If there is anything I have learned in my twenty-something years of lampshade design, it's that we all see beauty in different ways. In my early years, I used to become upset when friends or customers didn't like something I had very proudly made. I have now accepted the fact that everyone's taste is different and that our aesthetics evolve and develop, just as we do. Not everyone is as crazy about polka dots as I am, for instance. To add whimsy to whimsy, string some dangly beads on all four corners, an idea that was inspired by my love of glass bead earrings.

This fabric is similar to a sheeting fabric; it is very smooth on the wrong side. Often fabric at discount fabric stores has this same smooth side. If your fabric does, you may need to use a spray adhesive to properly laminate it to the styrene. Do so only in a very well-ventilated space. I use my ironing board as my work surface and lay a stack of newspaper on top of it. Each time I spray a panel, I flip a page of the newspaper. This keeps the work surface clean. Take care not to let the adhesive drip onto the fabric; it can ruin it!

TIP: Perform a test spray with the adhesive before using it to be sure it does not come out in splotches.

[1] Follow the instructions for the Basic Lampshade-Making Technique, pages 14–15, through step 6.

[2] Working with one panel at a time, remove the paper backing from the styrene, add spray adhesive onto the styrene (if necessary), and laminate it onto the back of the fabric as desired. Press with your hand to adhere. Do *not* iron; the styrene will melt. Flip the fabric over and look at it from the front to make sure your design is where you intended it to be. Cut out the panel.

[3] Follow steps 9–16 of the Basic Lampshade-Making Technique, pages 16–17.

[4] To make the "shade earrings" for each corner, use the needle and gold thread to thread the buttons and beads in an alternating pattern, making 4 strands of 8 beads and buttons each. When you've threaded the last button or bead, set aside.

[5] Adhere the vertical rib self-trim and grosgrain, following steps 18–20 of the Basic Lampshade-Making Technique, page 18. At each corner, sew an "earring" into the grosgrain and secure on the underside with a double knot. Allow the earrings to drop ½" to 1" (13mm–2.5cm) from the bottom of the shade.

[6] Add the rick-rack trim, gluing a few inches at a time.

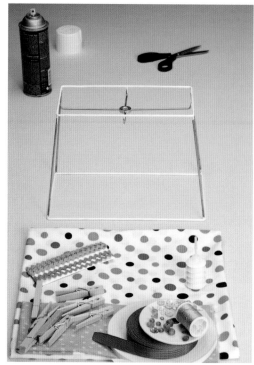

elements of the shade

steps 3–5

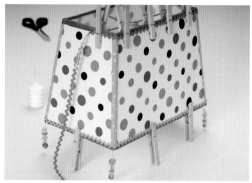

step 6

Favorite Nantucket
Cottage Shade

finished measurements

All materials are for a hexagonal bell washer-top shade measuring 7" (18cm) across the top x 12" (30.5cm) across the bottom x 8" (20.5cm) high. Adjust according to the size of your shade.

materials

½ yd (.45m) embroidered fabric

7" x 12" x 8" (18cm x 30.5cm x 20.5cm) hexagonal bell washer-top shade

½ yd (46cm) pressure-sensitive styrene

2 yd (1.8m) ⅝"- (16mm-) wide white cotton/rayon grosgrain ribbon

4 yd (3.7m) ¼"- or ⁵⁄₁₆"- (6mm- or 8mm-) wide pressure-sensitive cloth tape (bias-trim backer)

spray starch, optional

basic lampshade-making supplies (page 14)

Favorite Nantucket Cottage Shade

I first sold this shade at my beloved friend John Rugg's antique shop on India Street in Nantucket. John used to spend his winters in upstate New York and would come by my shop to drink tea and talk lampshades. How I miss him! He especially loved white on white embroidery like this one, which didn't surprise me because it is as elegant as he was. Indeed, it's the kind of shade one might find in the grand old shingled "cottages" that dot New England's coast and islands. And even though my shop is in the only landlocked state in the region, white-on-white embroidery shades are among the most popular, not least because you simply can't go wrong introducing one to almost any interior. They are especially ideal in a bedroom or a woman's home office.

I make all these shades from vintage white embroidery in cotton or linen. Tablecloths are perhaps the easiest to find; look for dresser scarves and table runners, too. You may find vintage embroideries with holes or stains; just work around them. That's one of the reasons I use vintage pieces on paneled shades—the amount of usable fabric needed is small.

TIP: Scorch marks can make you cry. I know. I have lots of experience with them. But I've had success removing the least angry ones by soaking them in tepid soapy water.

[1] Prepare the iron and ironing board. Turn the iron to the cotton/linen setting.

[2] Follow steps 1–4 of the Basic Lampshade-Making Technique, page 14, to cut out the styrene panels.

[3] On a clean work surface, lay the embroidery wrong side up. Working only on the part you will use, trim away loose threads or those that are carried from one embroidered spot to another so that they don't show through when the lamp is lit.

elements of the shade

[4] Iron the embroidery on the wrong side, taking care not to scorch it by keeping the iron moving. Use the spray starch, if desired, to stiffen cotton or linen.

[5] Follow steps 6–13 of the Basic Lampshade-Making Technique, pages 15–17. Arrange the panels in the order that you would like them on the shade. I prefer alternating a really busy pattern with a quiet one to give the shade a nice balance.

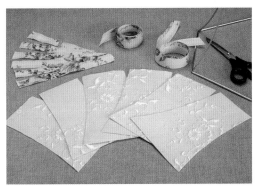

steps 5–6

[6] To make the top and bottom self-trims, use the 2 lengths of grosgrain as your guide to cut 2 lengths of the pressure-sensitive cloth tape. Laminate it to the wrong side of the fabric and cut out, adding ¼" (6mm) one each side of the tape and cutting flush to the tape on the ends. Proceed in the same manner for the vertical self trims.

step 7

[7] Complete assembly of the shade as in steps 16–21 of the Basic Lampshade-Making Technique, pages 17–18.

finished measurements

All materials are for a hexagonal bell shade measuring 8" (20.5cm) across the top x 14" (35.5cm) across the bottom x 9" (23cm) high. Adjust according to the size of your shade.

materials

½ yd (46cm) vintage or new cotton or linen toile

8" x 14" x 9" (20.5cm x 35.5cm x 23cm) hexagonal bell shade frame with washer top

½ yd (46cm) pressure-sensitive styrene

2 yd (1.8m) ⅝"- (16mm-) wide cotton/rayon grosgrain ribbon

4 yd (3.7yd) ¼"- or ⁵⁄₁₆"- (6mm- or 8mm-) wide pressure-sensitive tape (bias-trim backer)

¹⁄₁₆ yd (6cm) vintage or new cotton or linen toile, or raw linen for self-trim (optional)

basic lampshade-making supplies (page 14)

Antique Floral Toile Shade

Toile is typically found in classic interiors, most often in formal dining and living rooms. But my personal love for the fabric finds me using this two-color textile wherever and whenever I can. What's more, there are several manufacturers who make tongue-in-cheek toile fabrics based on the pastoral scenes so often associated with antique toiles.

Toile is very beautiful when it's lit; the color really pops when you turn on the switch. And what lights up is just magical—birds, florals, and leaves. My goal was to make these parts of the textile the major focus of the shade, so I designed each panel so that a bird or flower was highlighted. For this reason, paneled shades work very well with toile.

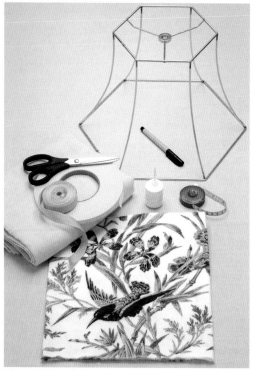

elements of the shade

steps 1–3

step 4

[1] Cut out the styrene panels following steps 1–4 of the Basic Lampshade-Making Technique, page 14.

[2] With the fabric wrong side up, iron it so that it is wrinkle free. Turn the fabric right side up and place it on a clean work surface. For this particular toile, in which birds play a starring role, I made mental notes on their placement in the pattern— I wanted to incorporate a large part of one on at least one panel rather than ending up with just the beak, say, or the tip of a wing! Really study the pattern on your toile—if it features a group of people sitting under a tree, try to incorporate the whole image onto a panel. Forget trying to "match" the panels, as would be done in upholstery; it will drive you crazy and really isn't necessary.

[3] Create the panels and secure them to the frame following steps 7–12 of the Basic Lampshade-Making Technique, pages 15–17.

[4] To make the self-trim, place the fabric wrong side up on a work surface. Lay the strips of cloth tape on the fabric. I have used raw linen instead of the toile for the self-trim on the top and bottom of the shade. Assemble and complete the shade following steps 13–20 of the Basic Lampshade-Making Technique, pages 17–20.

[5] To affix the decorative trim around the bottom of the shade, position it ¼" (6mm) above the grosgrain, beginning at the back of the shade, and, working in 3" (7.5cm) intervals, apply some glue along its length, press with your hands, and secure with clothespins. Trim the ends as above. For the decorative trim on the top rim, apply it as you did the grosgrain there.

A BRIEF HISTORY OF TOILE

Toile, which is the French word for "cloth," was first manufactured in Jouy-en-Josas, a village southwest of Paris near Versailles in the eighteenth century. It was made with block prints until the technology for copperplates was invented in the late 1700s. The factory in Jouy-en-Josas became famous for its monochromatic toiles—red, blue, or black floral and pastoral scenes printed on white or cream backgrounds—especially among French royalty, including Marie Antoinette. Indeed, the idyllic scenes of the French countryside and its people at leisure fit in with her idealized version of life. The upper classes, too, made great use of toile in their home decorating, filling rooms with draperies, bed hangings, pillows, and slipcovers. More than three centuries later, toile still shows up in interiors, sometimes filling a room from floor to ceiling but other times used sparingly on a pillow or two. No matter how you use it, toile remains timeless—and wholly appropriate almost anywhere in the house.

finished measurements

All materials are for a rectangular shade with washer measuring 9" x 7" (23cm x 18cm) across the top, 14" x 7" (35.5cm x 25.5cm) across the bottom, and 10½" (26.5cm) high. Adjust according to the size of your shade.

materials

1 vintage linen feed sack

9" x 7" (23cm x 18cm) on top x 14" x 10" (35.5cm x 25.5cm) on bottom x 10½" (26.5cm) high rectangular shade frame

1 yd (91cm) pressure-sensitive styrene

2½ yd (2.3m) ⅝"- (16mm-) wide cotton/rayon grosgrain ribbon in a complementary color

4 yd (3.7m) ⅝"- (16mm-) wide cotton/rayon grosgrain ribbon in muslin color

basic lampshade-making supplies (page 14)

Vintage Linen Grain Sack Shade

Grain sacks have long been the darlings of a certain kind of decorator—the type who loves an interior that's a little organic, a bit classic, and somewhat casual. I have seen them used as upholstery fabric time and again and as cushions, pillows, tableware, and window dressing. And why not? The sacks were made to last. The average age of a vintage linen grain sack is around one hundred years old, in fact. They're also mold- and mildew-resistant, which means a sack or two in the bathroom—as a hand towel, a bath mat, or, yes, a lampshade—is ideal.

You'll notice that I did not make self-trim from the linen for the vertical ribs. It's too thick and bulky to use that way. Your best bet is to find some grosgrain that closely matches the color of the sack. This shade strikes an original note; it combines both modern and classic sensibilities with superb results.

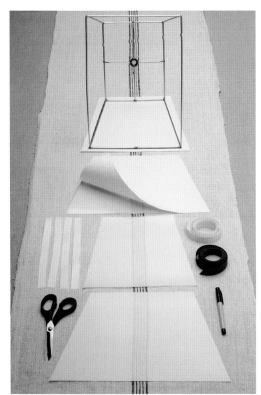

step 1

attaching the panels

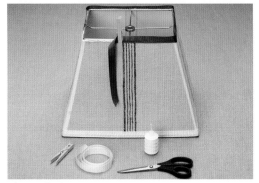

steps 3–4

[**1**] Follow the instructions for the Basic Lampshade-Making Technique, pages 14–17, through step 13. You will be cutting 2 each of 2 different-size panels.

[**2**] To make the vertical trim, cut four 10½" (26.5cm) lengths of the ⅝"- (16mm-) wide muslin-colored grosgrain. Run 3 very light beads of glue down the length of the grosgrain and place on the shade rib. Hand-press. Remove any excess glue with your finger. Repeat with the remaining ribs.

[**3**] Follow steps 18–20 of the Basic Lampshade-Making Technique, page 18, to apply the complementary-colored grosgrain around the top and bottom of the shade.

[**4**] Rather than add self-trim onto the grosgrain, simply glue a length of muslin-colored grosgrain flat along the edge of the shade (on top of the complementary-colored grosgrain). The colored grosgrain will be visible as it wraps around the top and bottom edges of the frame. Reverse the colors if desired.

finished measurements

All materials are for a hexagonal bell shade measuring 5" (12.5cm) across the top x 8" (20.5cm) across the bottom x 6" (15cm) high. Adjust according to the size of your shade.

materials

1 vintage floral tablecloth; 2 if you want to use different fabrics for the self-trims, as here

5" x 8" x 6" (12.5cm x 20.5cm x 15cm) galvanized hexagonal bell clip-top shade frame

½ yd (46cm) pressure-sensitive styrene

1½ yd (1.4m) ⅝" (15.9mm) wide cotton/rayon grosgrain ribbon

2½ yd (2.3cm) ¼"- or ⁵⁄₁₆"- (6mm- or 8mm-) pressure-sensitive cloth tape (bias-trim backer)

1 yd (91cm) pom-pom fringe for bottom

basic lampshade-making supplies (page 14)

1950s Kitchen Tablecloth Shade

Retro tablecloth designs are irresistible to me, perhaps because the color palette is so lovely—the bright aquas, yellows, reds, and eggshell blues are easy to incorporate into even the most neutral decor to wonderful effect. Lampshades covered in these cloths can't help but make you think about a simpler time. What's more, many feature strong borders that can be used for making self-trim around the top and bottom of the shade as well as for the ribs.

I often suggest to my customers that they put a lamp like this one on the kitchen counter or in a dining nook; it infuses even the slickest space with soul. Wall sconces are handy in the kitchen and are a good way to keep the shade away from tomato sauce.

TIP: Most tablecloths feature contrasting colors, which means that the design of your shade is practically done for you. Use the contrasting hue for the self-trim.

elements of the shade

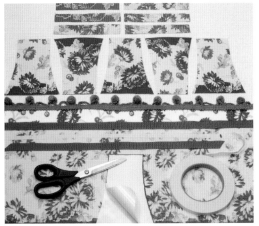

step 3

step 4

[1] Follow the Basic Lampshade-Making Technique, pages 14–15, through step 6.

[2] When deciding which parts of the tablecloth will become panels on the shade, consider alternating busy floral panels with those that feature fewer flowers and more background.

[3] Pick up with step 7 of the Basic Lampshade-Making Technique, page 15, through step 20.

[4] Add pom-pom trim around the bottom of the shade on top of the grosgrain, adding glue to the trim and adhering to the grosgrain, a few inches at a time, securing with clothespins. Alternative trims would include self-trim by itself, glass beads, onion tassels, or rickrack.

finished measurements

All materials are for a rectangular clip shade measuring 5" x 3" (12.5cm x 7.5cm) across the top, 9" x 6" (23cm x 15cm) across the bottom, and 6½" (16.5cm) high. Adjust according to the size of your shade.

materials

¼ yd (23cm) redwork embroidery

5" x 3" (12.5cm x 7.5cm) x 9" x 6" (23cm x 15cm) x 6½" (16.5cm) rectangular clip frame

½ yd (46cm) pressure-sensitive styrene

2 yd (1.8m) ⅝"- (16mm-) wide cotton/rayon grosgrain ribbon

2 yd (1.8m) ½"- (13mm-) wide vintage or new trim for the top and bottom of the shade

1 yd (91cm) ¼"–½"- (6mm–13mm-) wide vintage or new trim for vertical ribs

basic lampshade-making supplies (page 14)

Early Redwork Embroidery Shade

Redwork is embroidery stitched onto a white or off-white background with red thread (or another contrasting color). The stitching is often simple—there are no intricate designs, as in crewelwork—and the red thread typically used contrasts beautifully against the light background. Red is also prevalent because, during the nineteenth century, when redwork came into vogue, thread in this color was colorfast, unlike most other colors; it wouldn't wash out or bleed onto the white fabric.

You may come across old quilt squares, dresser scarves, tablecloths, or other miscellaneous vintage textiles that incorporate redwork. Some of these older pieces may be described as "turkey red." You might also notice that these pieces will be quite a bit pricier than red embroideries that are not so labeled. That's because turkey red is a natural dye from the root of the madder plant, used to color fabric.

TIP: Because redwork typically features large-scale designs of specific items, such as fruit, animals, or plants, I rarely use it to make the trim for the ribs of a shade. I generally choose a decorative ready-made trim like the one pictured.

elements of the shade

trim any loose threads

step 4

[1] You will be cutting 2 each of 2 different-size panels from the styrene for this rectangular shade. Lay the shade frame on its side, clip the styrene to it with the clothespins, and, with one hand behind the styrene, place pressure against the frame while tracing around it with a permanent marker. Using the marker lines as your guide, cut out each panel, adding about ½" (13mm) on all sides.

[2] Follow steps 2–13 of the Basic Lampshade-Making Technique, pages 14–17, to create the panels and begin the shade assembly.

[3] When the lampshade has dried, remove the grosgrain and clothespins. Trim away any excess styrene.

[4] To finish the shade, cut 2 lengths of the grosgrain ribbon, each 1" (2.5cm) longer than the circumference of the top and bottom of the shade. Cut one strip of decorative trim equal to the height of the shade for each rib on the shade. Attach the trim on the ribs and the grosgrain to the top and bottom of the shade, following steps 17–20 of the Basic Lampshade-Making Technique, pages 17–18.

[5] To apply the decorative trim around the top and bottom of the shade, work with 3" (7.5cm) of the trim at a time and begin at the center back of the shade. Apply glue to the trim and affix it directly over the grosgrain. Be careful not to apply too much glue. Scrape any excess away immediately. You may use clothespins to secure the trim in place, but do not leave them on too long, or they may make an indentations on the trim. Cut the ends of the trim on the diagonal so that they slightly overlap, and adhere with glue.

finished measurements

All materials are for a hexagonal washer-top shade measuring 6" (15cm) across the top x 12" (30.5cm) across the bottom x 8" (20.5cm) high. Adjust according to the size of your shade.

materials

½ yd (46cm) vintage or reproduction crewel fabric

8" x 12" x 6" hexagonal washer-top frame

½ yd (46cm) pressure-sensitive styrene

2 yd (1.8m) ⅝"- (16mm-) wide cotton/rayon grosgrain ribbon

1½ yd (1.4m) ¼"- or ⁵⁄₁₆" (6mm- or 8mm-) wide pressure-sensitive cloth tape (bias-trim backer)

2 yd (1.8m) French gimp or decorative braid for the top and bottom trim

basic lampshade-making supplies (page 14)

Grammy's Antique Crewel Shade

My grandmother Gulian was a crewel expert. Everywhere you looked in her house there was crewelwork covering something. Pillows, wall pieces, chairs—you name it. Surprisingly, I don't have a single piece of it to call my own! I was drawn to this crewelwork at an antiques show in New Hampshire for its unusual palette. I also love cream-on-cream crewels, especially if I'm making shades for a country interior. That said, they also work beautifully in a modern interior when using a contemporary-shaped frame. If you can't find a full piece of crewelwork, scraps can be cleverly used to cover a shade.

TIP: How do you choose the elements that go into a lampshade? Always consider the lamp base when choosing the shade frame. I used this hex washer frame because its classic shape fit with the pottery base. As for the French braid trim, it has a good weight to it, which stands up to the hefty crewelwork.

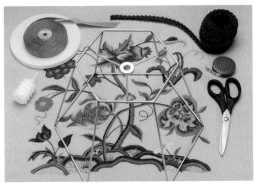

elements of the shade

step 4

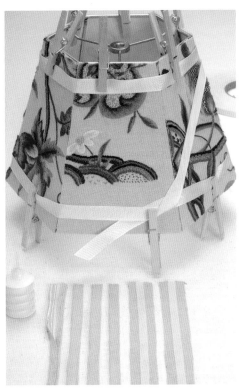

step 5

[1] Cut out the styrene panels, following steps 1–4 of the Basic Lampshade-Making Technique, page 14.

[2] With the fabric wrong side up, iron it so that it is wrinkle free. Trim away any loose threads or carried threads on the crewelwork. Take your time with this step, as any threads remaining will show through when you turn the light on.

[3] Turn the fabric right side up and place it on a clean work surface. Study the possibilities for your design. My piece of crewel fabric was not very large, so I had to carefully plan where to laminate the styrene, since there was little fabric to spare.

[4] Create the panels and secure them to the frame, following steps 7–12 of the Basic Lampshade-Making Technique, pages 15–17.

[5] If you're making the vertical ribs self-trim from the crewelwork fabric, place the fabric wrong side up on a work surface. Use the edge of the fabric that doesn't have any crewelwork on it to avoid bulky trims. Alternatively, choose a different, neutral fabric. Continue to create the self-trim, as in steps 14–15 of the Basic Lampshade-Making Technique, page 17.

[6] When the lampshade has dried, remove the grosgrain and clothespins. Trim away any excess styrene.

[7] Attach the vertical ribs self-trim and the grosgrain and pre-made trim around the top and bottom of the shade, following steps 17–21 of the Basic Lampshade-Making Technique, pages 17–18.

finished measurements

All materials are for a square bell washer-top shade measuring 6" (15cm) across the top x 10" (25.5cm) across the bottom x 8½" (21.5cm) high. Adjust according to the size of your shade.

materials

6" x 10" x 8½" (15cm x 25.5cm x 21.5cm) square bell washer-top frame

1 chenille bedspread or parts of one (about ½ yd [46cm] total for panels and 2 yd [1.8m] of edging of spread for shade trim)

½ yd (46cm) pressure-sensitive styrene

2 yd (1.8m) ⁵⁄₁₆"- (16mm-) wide cotton/rayon grosgrain ribbon

3 yd (2.75m) ¼"- or ⁵⁄₁₆"- (6mm- or 8mm-) wide pressure-sensitive cloth tape (bias-trim backer)

basic lampshade-making supplies (page 14)

Dreamy Creamy Chenille Shade

Chenille is the French word for "caterpillar," an apt way to describe the raised tufts of thread that form it. Of all the chenilles, I find the white on white and cream spreads to be my favorites. As shades, they're versatile enough to incorporate into rustic or refined interiors. Look for vintage chenille at flea markets, antique stores, estate sales, and on online auction sites. There are some great new chenilles out there, too.

TIP: Chenille is by nature rather thick, which means it can be a bit challenging to work with. Don't hesitate to trim the chenille a little if doing so makes it appear less bulky. I typically trim it if I'm using it for the self-trims.

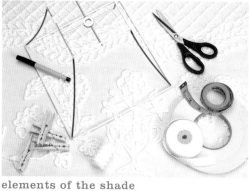

elements of the shade

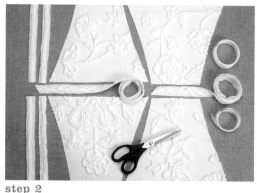

step 2

step 3

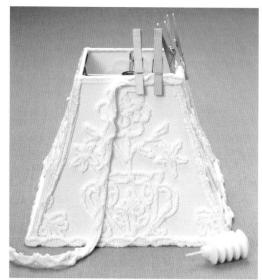

step 4

[1] Follow the instructions for the Basic Lampshade-Making Technique, page 14.

[2] When cutting out the fabric-covered panels in steps 7–8, if the thick chenille pattern runs along the edge of the panel, trim it back a bit by cutting it on an angle to reduce bulk when the panels come together.

[3] Fitting large shades perfectly can be harder than fitting smaller ones. In steps 10–11, be sure to fit and refit, taking your time, until the panels fit just right.

[4] When making the self-trims in step 14, look for lengths of repeated patterns on the chenille to cut from. Chenille often has nice strips of dots or long strips of straight chenille that are perfect for self-trims. When attaching them, use a generous amount of glue; chenille soaks it right up.

NOTE: If you don't have enough length for the trim, splice 2 pieces together. Begin by gluing the finished trim onto the grosgrain. Cut the end on a diagonal and continue with another piece, cut on the diagonal and overlapping the first slightly. Continue in this manner until the entire shade is trimmed.

finished measurements

All materials are for a hexagonal scallop shade measuring 4" (10cm) across the top x 8" (20.5cm) across the bottom x 6" (15cm) high. Adjust according to the size of your shade.

materials

4 yd (3.7m) antique quilt squares or quilting fabric in 6 different patterns

4" x 8" x 6" (10cm x 20.5cm x 15cm) hexagonal scallop frame

¼ yd (23cm) pressure-sensitive styrene

1½ yd (1.4m) ⅝"- (16mm-) wide cotton/rayon grosgrain ribbon

1½ yd (1.4m) ⁵⁄₁₆"- (8mm-) wide pressure-sensitive cloth tape (bias-trim backer)

⅛ yd (11cm) cotton fabric for vertical ribs and top trim

1 yd (91cm) ¼"- (6mm-) wide decorative trim for the bottom of the shade

basic lampshade-making supplies (page 14)

Antique Quilt Top Scalloped Shade

One person's unfinished quilt can be another's lampshade—at least, that's how I like to look at it. I become rather sentimental when I see vintage quilts only partly completed—the love and care and *work* that must have gone into them before life got too busy to get back to them. If you don't have antique quilt pieces, by all means purchase quilting fabrics new. You can either stitch them together into your own quilt top and cut the panels from them, or use a single different fabric on each panel. Try a polka dot self-trim for the vertical ribs or choose a calmer, more neutral fabric. Use the unexpected for a touch of whimsy; it works!

I have discovered in my classes that there are tassel people and no-tassel people. If you put yourself in the latter category, I urge you to give flirty trims a try on this shade. Scallops seem to love shirred trims like the one I use here—mini pom-poms or onion tassels are also great.

elements of the shade

step 2

step 4

applying the decorative trim

[1] Follow the instructions for the Basic Lampshade-Making Technique, page 14, through step 6. Think through your design carefully at this point so that each panel is different and no two patterns run consecutively from one panel onto the next. Also, with very old fabrics, such as quilt tops, it is essential to hold the fabric set on top of the styrene up to the light before cutting it out to ensure that there are no stains or spots.

[2] Resume with steps 7–9 of the Basic Lampshade-Making Technique, pages 15–16.

[3] When you reach step 10, refitting and recutting the panel to fit the frame, you may need to do it several times for this particular shade. It's a bit more challenging to achieve a perfect fit with the scallop shade.

[4] Continue assembly of the frame, following the Basic Lampshade-Making Technique, pages 16–18, through step 21.

country dotted swiss shade

materials

¼ yd (23cm) cotton dotted swiss fabric

4" x 8" x 6" (10cm x 20.5cm x 15cm) hexagonal scallop clip frame

¼ yd (23cm) pressure-sensitive styrene

1¼ yd (1.1m) ⅝"- (16mm-) wide cotton/rayon grosgrain ribbon

2¼ yd (2m) ¼"- or ⁵⁄₁₆"- (6mm- or 8mm-) wide pressure-sensitive cloth tape (bias-trim backer)

1 yd (91) mini pom-pom fringe for the bottom of the shade

basic lampshade-making supplies (page 14)

Dotted swiss fabric makes me think of an island cottage off the coast of Maine. I can imagine the windows open and the lightweight curtains blowing in the wind. Using dotted swiss on lampshades seems obvious for a summer bedroom, but that's not the only place this lovely textile can show off its numerous charms. It can be used to soften a room or serve as the inspiration for the decor in a nursery. It always looks good, of course, in a summer cottage. I used new dotted swiss, but there are lots of vintage versions out there; just look them over carefully and watch for stains and holes.

To make this shade, follow the instructions for the Antique Quilt Top Scalloped Shade, page 114, but be sure to keep the following in mind:

- Because the pattern of dotted swiss is exactly the same throughout, the trick for this fabric is to make sure the dots are aligned as you wish—straight up and down, or on the diagonal. Either way is fine, but if you want them perfectly straight in either direction, you must be very careful to place the styrene on the fabric just so.

- When applying the grosgrain to the scalloped bottom of this shade, give the grosgrain a pull and use a few extra clothespins to secure it to the shade. This will help to smooth any puckers.

finished measurements

All materials are for a square bell shade measuring 6" (15cm) across the top, 14" (35.5cm) across the bottom and 12" (30.5cm) high. Adjust according to the size of your shade.

materials

vintage cotton floral chenille bedspread

6" x 14" x 12" (15cm x 35.5cm x 30.5cm) square bell shade frame

1 yd (91cm) pressure-sensitive styrene

2½ (2.3m) yd ⅝"- (16mm-) wide cotton/rayon grosgrain ribbon

4 yd (3.7m) ¼"- or ⁵⁄₁₆"- (6mm- or 8mm-) wide pressure-sensitive cloth tape (bias-trim backer)

basic lampshade-making supplies (page 14)

Floral Chenille Shade

Vintage chenille bedspreads are ideal for turning into lampshades because they are often imperfect, either stained or full of holes or simply too threadbare to spread on a bed. To make them into shades, simply cut around these problems. Gently worn chenille spreads are quite common at flea markets and in antique shops. Modern designs and color choices can also be quite impressive and of good quality.

Large chenille patterns are best used on large shades like this one. The big patterns fit the larger-size shade panels. Some chenille has edging that is perfect for making self-trim, too, and using the same fabric for the self-trim makes for a perfect finish. I have also very successfully used onion tassels on chenille shades for the bottom trim of large square bell shades.

TIP: Chenille will take a little more glue and hand pressure when applying the vertical strips. Try to get a nice, tight seal with self-trims, if possible. It is helpful to let the glue dry a little and go back when it is tacky and press again.

step 2

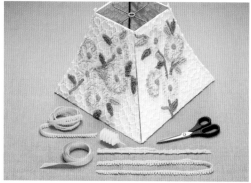

step 3

step 4

[1] Follow the instructions for the Basic Lampshade-Making Technique, pages 14–18.

[2] When cutting out the fabric-covered panels in steps 7–8, if the thick chenille pattern runs along the edge of the panel, trim it back a bit by cutting it on an angle to reduce bulk when the panels come together.

[3] In step 9, be sure to fit and refit, taking your time, until the panels fit just right. Panels on large shades are more time consuming and a little more challenging to fit nicely than those on smaller shades.

[4] When making the self-trims in step 14, look for lengths of repeated patterns on the chenille to cut from. Chenille often has nice strips of dots or long strips of straight chenille that are perfect for self-trims. When attaching them, use a generous amount of glue; chenille soaks it right up.

finished measurements

All materials are for a cut-corner rectangular bell shade measuring 7" x 5" (18cm x 12.5cm) across the top, 15" x 10" (38cm x 25.5cm) across the bottom, and 9½" (24cm) high. Adjust materials according to the size of your shade.

materials

large vintage embroidery tablecloth or several dresser scarves

7" x 5" (18cm x 12.5cm) x 15" x 10" (38cm x 25.5cm) x 9½" (24cm) galvanized cut-corner rectangular bell frame

½ yd (46cm) pressure-sensitive styrene

2 yd (1.8m) ⅝" (16mm-) wide cotton/rayon grosgrain ribbon

4½ (4.1m) yd ¼"- or ⁵⁄₁₆"- (6mm- or 8mm-) wide pressure-sensitive cloth tape (bias-trim backer), cut into eight 9½" (24cm) strips for the vertical ribs, the remaining for the top and bottom self-trims

1½ yd (1.4m) onion tassel fringe

basic lampshade-making supplies (page 14)

Whimsical Floral Embroidery Shade

Vintage fabrics may be hard to find these days, but I never have trouble turning up vintage embroideries like this one, which started life as a protective covering and pretty embellishment for a table. Before you go digging around at the flea market, though, check your own or your mother's attic first. I'm willing to bet you'll find one tucked away among other family heirlooms. Wherever one turns up, do not fret if it has holes or stains—just be sure there's enough usable fabric to cover the size shade you have in mind. If there isn't, do what I do: Find another fabric in a complementary color palette and alternate the designs on the shade panels.

For this particular shade, my fringe frenzy is obvious: I just couldn't help myself when I saw the onion tassel fringe applied on the bottom. I had felt the shape of the shade needed some zip, and that little embellishment did the trick. If you're not the fringe type but don't want to use self-trim, rickrack is always fun, but the choice is yours.

[1] Follow the instructions for the Basic Lampshade-Making Technique, pages 14–18. For this shade, you will cut 3 different-size styrene panels, one size for the front and back facing panels, a slightly smaller size for the side panels, and a yet smaller size for the corners. In all, you will need 2 panels for the front and back, 2 for the sides, 2 for the corners that arch to the right and 2 for the corners that arch to the left.

[2] When you reach step 6, determine the placement of the images on the embroidery on your shade. Think it through before making any cuts. For this shade, I chose to put the predominant design, a cottage, on the front of the shade.

[3] Continue following the Basic Lampshade-Making Technique, through step 20. If you choose to use a decorative trim on the bottom of the shade, as I did here, affix it to the grosgrain as you did the self-trim on the top.

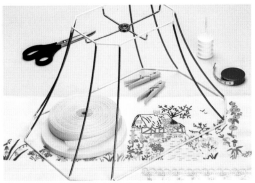

elements of the shade

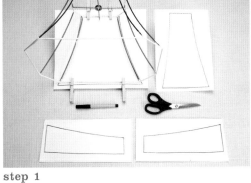

step 1

trim any loose threads

step 2

step 3

finished measurements

All materials are for a cut-corner square shade measuring 8" (20.5cm) across the top x 12" (30.5cm) across the bottom x 9" (23cm) high. Adjust according to the size of your shade.

materials

vintage needlepoint, or one that you've made yourself

8" x 12" x 9" (20.5cm x 30.5cm x 23cm) cut-corner square shade frame

½ yd (46cm) pressure-sensitive styrene

2½ yd (2.3m) ⅝" (15.9mm) wide cotton/rayon grosgrain ribbon

2 yd (1.8m) ¼"- or ⁵⁄₁₆"- (6mm- or 8mm-) pressure-sensitive cloth tape (bias-trim backer)

½ yd (46cm) cotton or linen fabric to complement the needlepoint

2½ yd (2.3m) decorative trim

basic lampshade-making supplies (page 14)

English Equestrian Needlepoint Shade

Needlepoint shades are a big hit in my shop. My customers want one-of-a-kind, high-design shades, and needlepoint certainly fits this description! Though needlepointing is still an active craft today, many of us may have greater access to pieces from the past. Needlepoint that our grandmothers or other loved ones have created often lies abandoned in attics and forgotten in dusty drawers just because we don't know how to incorporate it into our homes today. By turning these wonderful pieces of history into lampshades, you'll bring the past a little closer to the present.

Indeed I have to believe there are as many unfinished needlepoints in the world as there are people who love the craft. If you find one that isn't quite complete, you can certainly cut out panels around the missing parts. As with any lampshade, I chose the shade shape based on the size of the textile. Needlepoint may be a little bulky, but the size of this shade can handle the weight of it just fine. I used a neutral linen on the remaining panels so that the equestrian scene would be the focal point.

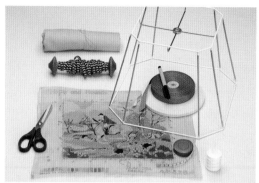
elements of the shade

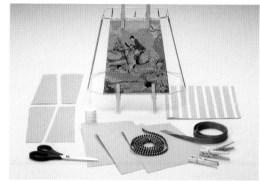
step 6

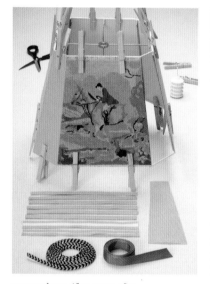
securing the panels

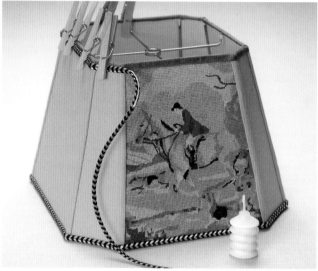
step 8

[1] For this shade, you will cut 2 different-size panels—that of the front, back, and sides and that of the corners. In all, you will cut out 4 panels of each; 8 panels total. Place the styrene sheet on a clean work surface. Lay the shade frame on its side and roughly trace around it with the permanent marker. Next, lay it on the corner and roughly trace around it with the permanent market. Using the marker lines as your guide, cut out the panel and corner, adding about ½" (13mm) on all sides.

[2] Clip a side panel to the frame at the top and bottom with 2 clothespins.

[3] Using the marker, trace the styrene along the exterior of the frame panel. This will give you a more precise measure of the panel. Cut out. Repeat steps 2 and 3 to make corner panels.

[4] Using the square side and corner panels as your templates, mark the styrene with 3 more of each. Cut out and set aside.

[5] With the fabric wrong side up, iron it so that it is wrinkle free. You may need to use steam if the needlepoint is a thick wool. Let it dry thoroughly before proceeding. Trim threads on the back of the needlepoint. Turn the fabric right side up and place it on a clean work surface. Decide which parts of the needlepoint you want where. Your favorite should go in the front!

[6] To create the panels and secure them to the frame, follow steps 7–12 of the Basic Lampshade-Making Technique, pages 15–17.

[7] Pick up with steps 13–17 of the Basic Lampshade-Making Technique, page 17, to make and apply the vertical ribs self trim and to cut the grosgrain. Don't even attempt to make self-trim from the needlepoint itself—it is impossible to work with when you're trying to manipulate it in such tight ways!

[8] Attach the grosgrain around the top and bottom of the shade's wires and then add the decorative trim, following steps 18–21 of the Basic Lampshade-Making Technique, page 18.

finished measurements

All materials are for a cut-corner square shade measuring 7" (18cm) across the top x 10" (25.5cm) across the bottom x 8" (20.5cm) high. Adjust according to the size of your shade.

materials

large vintage monogram tea towel

7" x 10" x 8" (18cm x 25.5cm x 20.5cm) cut-corner square shade frame

1 yd (91cm) pressure-sensitive styrene

2 yd (1.8m) ⅝"- (16mm-) wide cotton/rayon grosgrain ribbon

4 yd (3.7m) ⅜"- (9mm-) wide pressure-sensitive cloth tape (bias-trim backer), cut into nine 8" (20.5cm) lengths for the vertical and top trims, the remaining for the bottom self-trim

basic lampshade-making supplies (page 14)

Vintage Monogram Shade

A pair of these would make a lovely gift for newlyweds; the trick is finding their monogram—or even a single letter—on an old tea towel. If you come up short at the flea market or antique shop, do a search on online auction sites. The alternative is to have a monogram newly embroidered, which allows you to customize the lettering style. This tea towel has a decidedly French flair, and I can imagine it hanging from the oven handle in Madame's country kitchen. But when fitted on a lampshade, it takes on a wonderful cottage style.

> **TIP:** If you love a monogrammed tea towel that's too small to cover an entire shade, use huck cloth or linen in a similar weight to the towel for the back and/or sides.

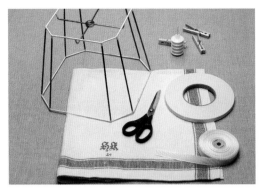

elements of the shade

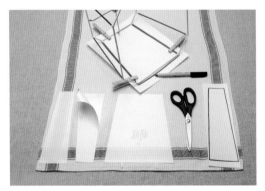

step 2

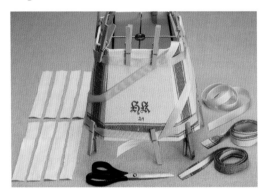

step 3

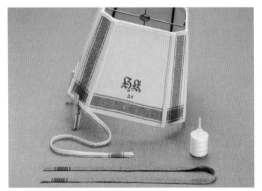

applying the self-trim

[1] Follow the instructions for the Basic Lampshade-Making Technique, pages 14–18. For this shade, you will cut 2 different-size styrene panels, one size for the large panels and one size for the corners.

[2] When you reach step 6, determine the placement of the monogram first. This will eliminate any chance of using up this section of the fabric for the other panels or corners. Think through where to place the styrene panels. Be as exacting as you can when adhering the styrene to the monogrammed panel; make a very light pencil mark on the panel on which you will place the monogram. I reserved the border of the tea towel for the corners and trim of my shade. Not all towels have a border, but I generally work with what I have. You can combine different linens, as long as the colors complement one another.

[3] Continue following the Basic Lampshade-Making Technique, through step 21.

Paisley Shawl Shade

finished measurements

All materials are for a hexagonal washer-top shade measuring 8" (20.5cm) across the top x 14" (35.5cm) across the bottom x 9" (23cm) high. Adjust according to the size of your shade.

materials

1 yd (91cm) antique wool paisley in good condition

8" x 14" x 9" (20.5cm x 35.5cm x 23cm) galvanized hexagonal washer-top shade frame

1 yd (91cm) pressure-sensitive paper

2½ yd (2.3m) ⅝"- (16mm-) wide cotton/rayon grosgrain ribbon in a complementary color

½ yd (46cm) complementary cotton trim

2½ yd (2.3m) gimp for the top and bottom trim

basic lampshade-making supplies (see page 14)

Paisley Shawl Shade

Some vintage paisley shawls are just waiting to be turned into shades, especially those that are no longer wearable. If a shawl has a moth hole or a stain, don't throw it out! Old paisley fabric is great for lampshades and is pretty easy to find, but somewhat tricky to work with. It can be very dry and brittle and more likely than not to be loaded with moth holes. These become a problem only if the entire piece of fabric is dotted with them. If you can work around them when laminating the pressure-sensitive paper to the fabric, you'll avoid an unpleasant surprise when you switch the light on: patches of holes! To prevent this from happening in the first place, hold the fabric up to a light and scrutinize it closely.

I prefer using pressure-sensitive *paper* instead of styrene when working with wool paisley. Although it allows less light through, the paper shows up the patterns on the paisley better when the light is on. With that in mind, use a paper-backed shade for decorative lighting rather than task or ambient light.

elements of the shade

step 1

step 2

step 3

[1] Follow the instructions for the Basic Lampshade-Making Technique, pages 14–17, through step 16, substituting pressure-sensitive paper for the styrene. Remember to closely inspect the fabric panels for moth holes after laminating by holding them up to the light.

[2] When attaching the vertical ribs, it is critical to use a fair amount of glue, since wool tends to be dry. Working on one vertical rib at a time, fold the cotton trim in half lengthwise to create a valley. Apply glue along the back side of the trim in the valley. Set the rib in place and hand-press it onto the shade.

[3] Follow steps 18–21 of the Basic Lampshade-Making Technique, page 18, to finish the shade.

TIPS: A friend swears by this method for ridding old wool fabrics, such as paisley, of moth eggs: Put the fabric in the freezer overnight and voilà, no more pests.

• Antique paisley makes nice shades in amost any shape except the bell shapes; their belled panels cause the fabric to sag.

• For the ribs on this shade, I used a cotton trim that very closely matches the wool rather than using the wool itself, which is too thick and challenging to glue onto the slender tape.

finished measurements

All materials are for a hexagonal scallop clip lampshade measuring 4" (10cm) across the top x 8" (20.5cm) across the bottom x 6" (15cm) high. Adjust according to the size of your shade.

materials

¼ yd (23cm) vintage or reproduction French cotton fabric, gently washed

4" x 8" x 6" (10cm x 20.5cm x 15cm) hexagonal scallop clip frame

¼ yd (23cm) pressure-sensitive styrene

1¼ yd (1.1m) ⅝"- (16mm-) wide cotton/rayon grosgrain ribbon

1 yard (91cm) ¼"- or ⁵⁄₁₆"- (6mm- or 8mm-) wide pressure-sensitive cloth tape (bias-trim backer)

1¼ yd (1.1m) French gimp or other decorative trim

basic lampshade-making supplies (page 14)

To-Die-For French Fabric Shade

Of all the vintage fabrics I have stashed away, the pretty, soft, faded French ones are among my favorites. There's something about the dyes and how they fade that makes them irresistible to me. Where to find these pretty French treasures? It is getting harder, but keep an eye on online auction sites or your favorite textile websites. I tend to find small tidbits of fabric, but once in a while, I land on a nice big piece.

If you find that there's just enough fabric for the lampshade panels and not the trim, simply use a pre-made trim or make the trim out of a contrasting fabric. I used a French gimp on this shade, but it would also look great with a delicate onion tassel fringe.

TIP: Use a few extra clothespins when adding the grosgrain ribbon to the bottom of the shade, and tug the ribbon as you work around the scallops.

[1] To make the panels, follow steps 1–4 of the Basic Lampshade-Making Technique, page 14.

[2] With the fabric wrong side up, iron it so that it is wrinkle free. Because I chose a very lightweight cotton, similar to that of a handkerchief, I used a little starch to stiffen it a bit. This helps to keep it straight when laminating. Continue assembly of the shade, creating and securing the panels following steps 6–13 of the Basic Lampshade-Making Technique, pages 15–17, then making the self-trims as in steps 14–15.

[3] When the lampshade has dried, remove the grosgrain and clothespins. Trim away any excess styrene.

[4] Affix the self-trim to the ribs and the grosgrain and self-trim around the top and bottom of the shade following steps 17–21 of the Basic Lampshade-Making Technique, pages 17–18.

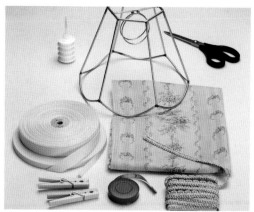

elements of the shade

step 2

step 4

european duvet shade

materials

¼ yd (23cm) antique European cotton duvet fabric or new floral cotton 4" x 8" x 6" (10cm x 20.5cm x 15cm) hexagonal scallop clip shade frame

¼ yd (23cm) pressure-sensitive styrene

1½ yd (1.4m) ⅝"- (16mm-) wide cotton/rayon grosgrain ribbon

1 yd (91cm) ¼"- or ⁵⁄₁₆"- (6mm- or 8mm-) wide pressure-sensitive cloth tape (bias-trim backer)

¼ yd (23cm) gingham cotton for self-trim on vertical ribs

1½ yd (1.4m) dresser scarf trim for the top and bottom of the shade

basic lampshade-making supplies (page 14)

French fabrics aren't the only kind "to die for." Type "vintage German fabrics" into the search engine on online auction sites and you will find a very pretty selection of floral cotton bedding that conjures images of European mountain and lakeside cottages. The patterns are sweet, but there is a sophistication about them, too—when you put a shade made from one in a room, it lends a bit of old-world flavor. A duvet cover will make lots of shades and perhaps some decorative bedroom pillows—a nice touch if you're inclined—or you may find some ready-made pillows in a matching fabric. I've suggested using gingham fabric for the vertical self-trim, another great way to match the shade to the rest of the room. You should be able to find coordinating pillows and linens in this popular print.

To make this shade, follow the instructions for the To-Die-For French Fabric Shade, page 134, but be sure to keep the following in mind:

- For the trim at the top and bottom of this shade, I used the edges of a dresser scarf. Cut the scarf ⅛" (3mm) from the embroidery edge. You may have to splice pieces of a scarf's edges together to have enough for the whole shade. Fold the ⅛" (3mm) of fabric back onto the wrong side of the edging and glue it down.

- Use gingham, cut on the bias, for the vertical self-trim.

lamps and finials

Now that you've mastered the art of making lampshades, why not move on to the lamps themselves? That's the question I asked myself so many years ago as my space began to fill up with shades—there weren't enough bases in town to hold them up! But seriously, if I must admit it, I began making my own lamps because I kept finding cool parts at flea markets from which to put them together. Once I began dismantling broken bases for parts and reviving them, a world of possibilities opened up. In the same way that I see lampshade ideas wherever I go, I began to design bases out of everything from cowboy boots to baby blocks.

As whimsical as a lamp may be, there are some lamp parts that are essential, no matter what lamp you create. Each one begins with a base, a threaded rod, a lamp socket, and a cord, and may feature far more pieces, including necks, plates, mirrored lamp parts, and more.

Lone RANGER

level: intermediate

materials

child-size cowboy boot

6" x 8" (15cm x 20.5cm) rectangular wood lamp base with drilled cord way

9" (23cm) threaded brass rod

1 or more brass necks (also known as spacers), enough to raise the socket just above the top of the boot, about 2" (5cm)

brass-plated check ring

brass lamp socket with bottom outlet

2 locknuts, one each for top and bottom

threadlocker

box of plaster of paris

wide-mouth funnel

small bucket or plastic yogurt or ice cream container

small piece of linen or leather to cover the plaster of paris at the boot opening, about 3" (7.5cm), square depending on size of boot

wooden paint stick for stirring

hand drill and $\frac{7}{16}$" (11mm) drill bit to fit threaded rod

vice to hold blocks for drilling

protective eyewear

dish towel

masking tape

stain or paint for base

wire stripper (optional)

8' (2.4m) clear electric cord

Duncan's Cowboy-Boot Lamp

For those of you who aren't the type to bronze your child's booties, here's a perfect way to preserve a tiny cowboy boot for posterity. Whenever I catch a glimpse of this lamp, I am immediately taken back to my son Duncan's childhood. The scuffed toes, the sound of the heels on the kitchen floor, the fringed vest!

I often find that boys' bedroom accessories are sorely lacking; it seems that girls get all the cool stuff! I guess this lamp, then, was a case of necessity being the mother of invention. That's not to say that it wouldn't be perfect in your favorite cowgirl's room, though. Top it off with a cowboy-themed lampshade or French ticking. I found this cowboy scarf at a flea market and used red bandanna fabric for the trim. A shade in either cotton or linen works best.

For this lamp, I chose to have the cord come out of the boot rather than using the simpler version in which the cord emerges from the socket. The wood lamp base is available at lighting supply stores or craft stores (Resources, page 156).

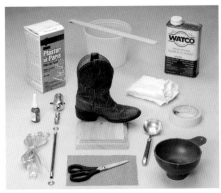
elements of the lamp

step 2

[1] Apply a coat of stain or paint on the lamp base. Let it dry overnight or follow manufacturer's instructions.

[2] Remove the insole of the boot. Wrap the boot in a dish towel and place it in the vice, using wooden blocks to hold the boot in place. Wearing protective eyewear, drill a hole vertically in the boot bottom; I positioned mine as close to the heel as I could so that there was space for the cord to come out.

[3] Align the hole in the boot with the hole in the lamp base. Slide the rod into the boot and through the base. Secure with the locknut on the inside bottom of the boot. Tighten. Seal off the area around the threaded rod on the bottom of the boot with masking tape; this will prevent the plaster of paris from leaking out. Wrap the rod exposed at the top of the lamp base with masking tape to prevent it from becoming covered with the plaster of paris.

[4] In the plastic container, add 2 parts plaster of paris to 1 part water and stir for 15 minutes or until the mixture has the consistency of sour cream. Place the funnel into the boot and pour the plaster of paris through it. Stop pouring when the plaster is about 1" below the lowest opening at the top of the boot. Work quickly, as the plaster sets quickly. Use the stirrer to release any air bubbles. Scrape off the plaster at the lip near the top of the boot and smooth the top with the stirrer. Let it dry overnight.

[5] Remove the masking tape from the top of the rod. Cut a hole about the size of the rod in the center of the small piece of fabric, and thread the fabric onto the rod. Turn the edges under to fit the boot opening; the fabric should sit snugly against the inside edge of the boot.

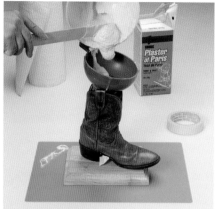

step 4

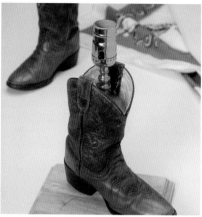

step 9

[6] Slip the check ring onto the threaded rod, followed by the brass necks. Leave about ¼" (6mm) at the top of the rod for the socket. You may need to make adjustments, depending on the height of your lamp; add as many brass necks as needed to cover the threaded rod. Conversely, use fewer if your lamp is a little shorter.

[7] Apply a few drops of threadlocker to the top of the rod and screw the bottom, or cap, of the socket onto the threaded rod. Run the cord through the threaded rod and out through the cap.

[8] Pick up the inside of the socket, called the push-thru interior. To wire the lamp, examine the two wires in the end of the cord that goes through the boot. Wrap the wire from the ribbed side of the cord around the nickel screw on the push-thru socket and tighten. Wrap the wire from the smooth side around the brass screw and tighten. (You may need to pull the two wires slightly apart and strip the plastic insulation from the cord to do this.)

[9] Set the top of the socket, or shell, in place; you will hear two clicks when it is properly in place.

[10] Tighten the locknut screw underneath the bottom of the base to securely tighten all the components of the lamp. Give the boot a nice polish and turn it on!

FOR THE SHADE

I found several vintage cowboy bandannas at a flea market—just the ticket for this base, which is a square bell measuring 4" (10cm) across the top x 7" (18cm) across the bottom x 7" (18cm) high. Follow the instructions for the Country Candlewicking Shade, page 63, to make the shade shown here.

vintage ski boot lamp

materials

ski boot

7" (18cm) brass or steel threaded rod for a child's boot, longer for an adult boot

three ½" (13mm) brass necks, or enough to fill the space between the boot and the socket

prewired lamp socket with side outlet

threaded brass locknut

threadlocker

small bag of plaster of paris

wide-mouth funnel

small bucket

small piece of fabric or leather to cover plaster of paris at the boot opening, about 6" (15cm)

wooden paint stirrer

If cowboys don't jump-start imaginations in your home, consider adapting the lamp to fit whatever interests do. This old-fashioned leather ski boot would make a great piece for a ski condo or a budding downhiller.

To make this lamp, follow the instructions for Duncan's Cowboy-Boot Lamp, page 139, but be sure to keep the following in mind:

- No drilling is necessary for this variation. Instead, place the funnel into the opening in the ski boot and pour the plaster of paris mixture into the funnel. Shake the boot gently as it begins to fill to release any air bubbles. Fill the boot to within 1" (2.5cm) from the top. Set the bucket aside and quickly set the threaded rod into the center of the boot opening, making sure it goes all the way to the bottom. The plaster of paris sets rather suddenly, so work quickly. When the mixture is set, place the fabric in place over the rod and turn under the edges. The edge will settle into the tacky plaster of paris. Let it dry overnight.

- Use a prewired side-outlet brass socket to make assembly easy.

level: intermediate

materials

5 vintage or new wooden blocks, the larger the better, plus more to decorate the base of the lamp

wood lamp base with drilled cord way (Resources, page 156)

10" (25.5cm) threaded metal rod (fits 5 blocks, about 2" (5cm) square)

3" to 4½" (7.5cm–11.5cm) brass necks, if you need to fill space

socket with bottom outlet (cord goes through lamp instead of out the socket)

brass locknut

threadlocker

hand drill and ⁷⁄₁₆" (11mm) drill bit

screwdriver

vice to hold blocks for drilling

stain or paint for base

wood glue

lamp cord set

Vintage Baby Blocks Lamp

My friend Lauren seems to go to more baby showers than there are babies born in this small corner of Vermont. It seems she's always coming by the shop to make one of these for an upcoming celebration, which is just fine with me, since I'm nuts about them. And who wouldn't be? They're an instant heirloom, not to mention practical and pretty.

[1] Paint or stain the base and let it dry.

[2] Using the drill and drill bit, drill holes through the center of the blocks to be threaded onto the rod.

[3] Screw the locknut to the end of the threaded rod and run the rod through the wooden base, with the locknut underneath the base.

TIP: Tape the 2 wires on the cord together with a piece of duct tape before you thread them through the rod; this helps to push them through with ease.

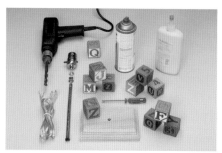

elements of the lamp

step 2

step 6

[4] Thread the blocks onto the rod in your preferred order. If some of the rod shows after threading all of the blocks onto it, use the brass necks to cover it. Add a threaded nut at the top of the rod, leaving just enough room to screw on the bottom, or cap, of the socket. Apply a few drops of thread lock to the rod and screw the cap onto the end of the threaded rod. Tighten to secure.

[5] Run the wire end of the cord through the lamp base and out through the threaded rod.

[6] The wires from the cord attach to the two screws on the lamp socket. Wrap the smooth-side wire onto the brass screw on the socket; wrap the ribbed-side wire onto the nickel screw on the socket. Tighten to secure.

[7] Add the shell, or top part, of the socket. Set it in place over the inside push-thru socket and push it down into the bottom cap of the socket. Listen for two clicks, a signal that it is securely in place.

[8] Arrange the remaining blocks on the lamp base and adhere with wood glue.

FOR THE SHADE

The rectangular shape of this base calls for a rectangular shade. I used a midsize one, just a little wider than the lamp base and just high enough to balance the lamp's height. I used a bold geometric fabric complemented by two different-color rickrack trims to let the lamp shine! Follow the instructions for the Cool Cottage Flowers Shade, page 60, to make this one.

level: easy

materials

antique or reproduction
kerosene lamp

wired socket with side
outlet

solid-brass adapter with
#1 brass nipple for a lamp
with a ¾" (2cm) opening
or #2 brass nipple for
heavier, larger lamps

threadlocker

Electrified Kerosene Lamp

As much as I appreciate the beauty of a working (or even nonworking!)
kerosene lamp, I've taken to electrifying them for the sake of conve-
nience. Converting them is surprisingly easy, and the parts are readily
available at quality lighting stores as well as at online lamp parts suppliers (Resources, page 156).

I love the look of vintage embroideries on kerosene shades, particularly when they are hexagonal or hexagonal bell shaped. Follow the
instructions for the Favorite Nantucket Cottage Shade, page 91, to make
one for this lamp.

[1] If the kerosene lamp has a burner, unscrew it
from the base.

[2] Thread the brass nipple into the socket, adding a touch of threadlocker to keep the lamp from
coming unscrewed. Add the #1 or #2 adapter followed by a small amount of threadlocker around
the circumference of the adapter. Screw the whole
piece into the opening on top of the lamp.

[3] Screw the whole piece into the opening on
top of the lamp.

NOTE: Do not drill valuable kerosene lamps. They may
crack and will certainly lose their value.

level: easy

materials

depression glass parts

10" (25.5cm) threaded brass or steel rod

4 new or gently used brass necks or spacers

7 or 8 check rings with 1⅛" (2.9cm) seat x ⅛ IP slip (hole size; fits standard threaded rod)

Socket with push-thru interior and bottom outlet

2 locknuts

threadlocker (keeps the lamp from unscrewing)

8 ft (2.5m) clear cord

vintage pushpin finials

curtain pushpins

glass/metal glue or 2-part epoxy

brass finial bases with swivel tops

Depression Glass Parts Lamp

Over the years, I have purchased untold numbers of Depression glass lamps. They seem to be everywhere, which is a good thing because an abundance keeps prices low. I occasionally will buy a Depression glass lamp that I don't particularly love or doesn't look quite right if I'm attracted to some of its parts. I simply take it apart and stash the pretty pieces for a future lamp.

Keep an eye out for old glass parts and cool mirror parts, also commonly used in Depression glass lamps. I like to mix them on a lamp and sometimes add aged parts and vintage sockets to keep the look cohesive. That said, I have found that mixing new lamp parts with old achieves a unique look, too. New parts are readily available at lighting supply stores and in lighting catalogs (Resources, page 156).

Whenever I buy vintage glass lamps, I always cut off the cords and replace the insides of the lamp. If the socket is in good shape, I like to keep the exterior. By saving the outside of the socket, you will preserve the vintage look of the lamp while adding a new interior, which makes it safer to use. In general, most lamps should be completely rewired if you buy them at a flea market or the equivalent.

Putting a glass lamp together takes some practice. The most important thing to remember is to use a check ring with each part. It sandwiches each glass part; place one check ring on the bottom of the glass part and one check ring on the top. Also, use plenty of brass necks or spacers. The bottom piece of glass must be good and sturdy, and it should be bigger than the other parts to be a base. I used a mirrored piece on top of the base shown here for a decorative addition.

TIP: A 10" (25.5cm) threaded rod is ideal for simple-to-make lamps; any taller and you'll need to add a harp, which is a more advanced lamp-making part.

[1] I made the lamp pictured here putting the following pieces together in this order: Begin with a locknut followed by the glass base, a flat round mirror, a check ring, a neck, another check ring, a glass part, a check ring, a neck, a check ring, and so on to the top of the rod. Thread the remaining locknut on top.

[2] Add a few drops of lockthread onto the threaded rod, then screw on the bottom part of the socket.

[3] Thread the cord through the bottom of the lamp and up through to the bottom cap.

[4] The lamp cord has a plug on one end and 2 wires on the other, one smooth, one ribbed. Wrap the wire from the smooth side around the brass screw on the socket and tighten; wrap the wire from ribbed side around the nickel screw on the socket. Tighten to secure. (You may need to pull the 2 wires slightly apart and strip the plastic insulation from the cord to do this.)

[5] Add the shell or top part of the brass socket. Set it in place over the inside push-thru socket and push down into the bottom cap of the socket. Listen for two clicks, a signal that it is securely in place.

vintage pushpin finials

The finial featured on the Depression Glass Parts Lamp is one of my favorites, a vintage curtain pushpin. Commonly crafted from Bakelite™, glass, or metal, this type of pushpin was used to hold back curtains as well as to hang artwork. The small pins in the curtain pushpin used here fit perfectly into the swivel on a brass finial top and therefore makes an ideal decorative finial.

[1] Squeeze a bit of glass/metal glue or spread prepared 2-part epoxy onto the top of one of the brass finial swivel tops.

[2] Set a pushpin into the glue, and let it dry overnight.

[3] Repeat with any remaining pushpins, if desired.

step 1

level: easy

materials
insert for a candelabra-style
lightbulb or regular-sized
lightbulb

2-part epoxy

masking tape

Candlestick Lamp

With the addition of an insert, you can turn almost any candlestick into a lamp, which is great news for those of us who seem to end up with single candlesticks over the course of time. Be sure to use candlesticks that are sturdy and solid, since they will be holding a lampshade.

The inserts for a standard lightbulb are called electrified candlestick and bottle adapters. They fit a variety of different candlestick sizes. Those for candelabra bulbs are known as wired candlestick kits. Both are available as kits online or at quality lighting supply shops.

[1] Check the fit of the corrugated rubber base of the insert with your candlestick, trimming down for a snug fit if necessary.

[2] Prepare the epoxy by squeezing equal amounts from each tube onto a piece of scrap cardboard and mixing them together.

[3] Spread a thin layer of epoxy around the corrugated rubber and insert it into the candlestick. Let dry overnight or according to the manufacturer's instructions.

finials

materials

glass/metal glue or 2-part epoxy

brass finial bases with swivel tops

antique or new marbles, the bigger the better

flat buttons, if necessary

sandpaper (optional)

Small found objects

Finials are used on the top of medium to large lamps to hold their shades in place (small lamps typically feature clip shades, which clip onto the lightbulb). The first finial project, shown here, the Big Marble, was inspired by the crystal balls that often hang from chandeliers. The second, the Found Object (page 118), came out of another *Aha!* moment. Once I realized that I could use a flat button as the base for rounded or off-kilter items, I knew there was no limit to what little treasures could become the perfect finial for a favorite lamp.

big marble

[1] Rough up the curve of the marble that will be set into the finial base by rubbing it with sandpaper or on pavement or a similar surface to promote adhesion.

[2] Working quickly, mix 2-part epoxy according to the manufacturer's instructions.

[3] Swab some epoxy into the brass finial base. Set the roughened side of the marble into the glue. Set aside to dry thoroughly overnight.

found objects

[1] If you're using 2-part epoxy, prepare it according to the manufacturer's instructions.

[2] Squeeze glue or dab epoxy onto the top of the brass finial swivel top. If necessary, glue a flat button to the finial swivel top first, let it dry, and then squeeze glue onto this button.

[3] Set the small found object into the glue and let it dry overnight.

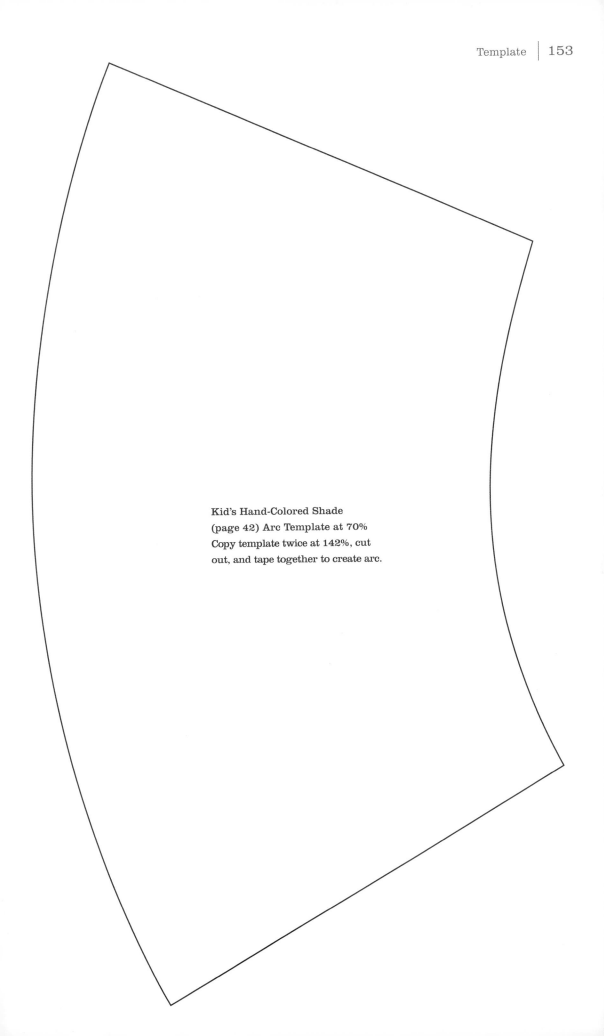

Kid's Hand-Colored Shade
(page 42) Arc Template at 70%
Copy template twice at 142%, cut
out, and tape together to create arc.

Glossary

Ambient lighting Light that floods a room, as opposed to decorative and task lighting, which are designed to shine in specific spaces.

Arc The pattern used for making empire, drum, and coolie shades. Available at lampshade supply stores (Resources, page 156).

Back seam clamp Wood clamp used to help secure the back seam of empire, coolie, and drum shades.

Beaded-steel brass plate A thin round brass lamp part that is used to cushion glass parts in lamp-making.

Bottle adapter kit A package containing all of the parts needed to make a candlestick lamp with a regular lightbulb.

Brass neck Also called a spacer, this part is used to top off the stem of a lamp base. Available threaded or can be slipped onto a threaded rod.

Candelabra lightbulb Flame-shaped bulb often used in wall sconces and chandeliers.

CFL The most common abbreviation for a compact fluorescent lightbulb; energy efficient lightbulbs.

Check ring A flat brass ring slid onto the lamp rod.

Chimney The glass hurricane used in kerosene lamps.

Clip adapter An attachment that converts a washer-top shade into a clip-top shade.

Clip top A frame designed to clip onto a lightbulb.

Clothespins The wooden variety is essential for holding the laminated panels in place during the lampshade-making process.

Cord set A lamp cord in which the plug is intact.

Decorative lighting Includes accent and task lighting, it is designed to draw attention to a specific area, such as a painting, bookshelf, mantle, or sofa table.

Diffuser A plastic insert placed on the top and/or bottom of a drum shade hung as a pendant lamp; used to hide the fixtures and the bulb.

Finial A decorative ornament secured on the top of a lamp; can be a conventional finial, designed for the purpose or can be made from found objects such as marbles or metal curtain pushpins.

Finial reducer An attachment that screws into the inside of a finial to reduce the size of its opening.

Finial swivel (concave top) A brass base onto which almost anything can be glued to create a finial.

Grosgrain ribbon Used in the processes of both making lampshades and embellishing them. *Always* use a cotton/rayon blend when making shades.

Hard-back shade A style of lampshade in which fabric or paper is laminated onto pressure-sensitive styrene or paper.

Harp A brass shade attachment that is secured below the lamp socket into the harp wings. Available in 4" to 14" (10cm–35.5cm) heights, regular and heavyweight. Old lamps often have a fixed harp: one piece that is attached below the socket. To replace fixed harps—if the lamp is from 1950 or earlier, when excessively tall harps were de rigueur, chances are you will want to—the socket must be removed.

Harp wings The brass piece below the socket that the harp clips into. Be sure that their sizes are compatible. They come in regular and heavy-duty.

Hurricane lamp Another name for a kerosene lamp, referring to the glass chimney that is an integral part of it.

Incandescent light The light we love for the warm glow it casts.

Lamp base Typically comes in wood or stone and used to build a lamp upon. The easiest to use are those with a drilled cord way, in which the cord comes out on the side of the base.

Locknut The part that holds all of the lamp parts together; one is screwed onto the threaded rod on the top and another on the bottom of the lamp.

No-thread uno A shade top that generally has a 4" (10cm) drop and sets onto the light socket before the lightbulb is screwed in.

Pressure-sensitive cloth tape Also known as bias-trim backer, a cloth tape that is sticky on one side. It is used in making self-trims. It can also be used to cover the inside wires of a shade frame. It is available in ¼" and ⁵⁄₁₆" (6mm and 8mm) widths.

Pressure-sensitive styrene The lampshade-maker's main ingredient. Plastic material that is smooth on one side and has a sticky adhesive on the other. Peel the paper off, set the adhesive side onto fabric, and hand-press.

Pressure-sensitive paper Similar to the styrene but a heavy paper instead of plastic. It is less translucent than the pressure-sensitive styrene, which makes it good for paisley and other fabrics that show up better with less light.

Pull-chain socket A lamp socket with a brass chain as the switch, handy for tall brass lamps and a nice decorative touch.

Push-thru socket My socket of choice! I prefer solid-brass sockets to gilt brass; they are much sturdier and fit together better. They're slightly more expensive but well worth the cost.

Quick glue A quick-dry craft glue that dries clear. I buy it by the gallon (Resources, page 156), transfer it into a smaller bottle, and then put it into squeeze bottles.

Scissors A basic lampshade-making tool used to cut pressure-sensitive styrene. I favor the Gingher® brand; their lightweight scissors are balanced perfectly for me, and they can be sent to the manufacturer for sharpening. Finding the right scissors is much like finding knives you are comfortable using. Hold them in your hand to get a feel for them.

Shell The exterior of a brass socket and the part that clicks into the bottom cap of the socket.

Socket Also known as the Edison socket, designed by Thomas Edison in 1881, it is the part of the lamp into which the lightbulb is screwed.

Soft-back shade Lined all-fabric shades typically made from silk or rayon.

Soutache A subtle finishing trim that gives a shade a crisp look without adding too much of a decorative element.

Spray adhesive Used only occasionally to achieve a solid lamination, especially with fabrics that have a smooth back and do not laminate easily.

Squeeze bottle A 2-ounce (59ml) plastic accordion-shaped bottle from which quick glue is easily dispensed. The bottle has a nipple on the end that makes it easy to run thin beads of glue for adhering trim. Refill the bottle by pulling the nipple out with needle nose pliers.

Task lighting Focused light designed to strongly illuminate a specific area in which work takes place.

Threaded rod A brass or steel rod that acts as the spine of a lamp; it runs through the base. It can be up to 36" (91cm) long.

Threadlocker An adhesive used when a strong bond is needed. A few drops is all you need to keep a lampshade together.

Uno adapter Converts a washer-top lamp into an uno-top lamp.

Uno shade frame and socket Fits onto a bridge, or floor, lamp. With this type of frame and socket, the lightbulb hangs down into the shade.

Resources

All basic lampshade materials are readily available at the sources I've listed here, and you'll also find sources for lamp parts and finials. This section includes sources that I regularly use, but you will find many other valuable sources online and will find many supplies at your local hardware, lighting, craft, and fabric stores.

Lampshade Supplies

At the time of publication, there are not many brick-and-mortar stores selling lampshade supplies. As a result, I have become accustomed to ordering materials over the phone, by fax, or via the Internet. The suppliers are typically very helpful and the shipping times relatively short.

Artistic Bias Products
1905 Elizabeth Avenue
Rahway, NJ 07065
732-382-4141
You can order pressure-sensitive styrene, pressure-sensitive cloth tape, pressure-sensitive vinyl, lampshade wrap, soutache, prelaminated styrene, and more.

Fogg Lighting
281 Marginal Way
Portland, ME 04101
207-797-7568
www.fogglighting.com
Fogg Lighting (formerly Mainely Shades) sells everything from lamp parts to lampshade-making supplies.

The Lamp Shop
P.O. Box 3606
Concord, NH 03302
603-224-1603
www.lampshop.com
As the name suggests, this retailer sells it all—every lamp part and lampshade-making supply you could want. Visit lampfinials.com for a complete source of finials.
P.O. Box 36
Concord, NH 03302
512-693-0888
www.lampfinials.com

Schiff Ribbons
215-538-2880
www.schiffribbons.com
This is a good resource for fine-quality woven-edge grosgrain.

W. N. de Sherbinin Products
P.O. Box 63
Hawleyville, Connecticut 06440
800-458-0010
www.wndesherbinin.com
This is a good place to find lamp parts.

New Fabric, Trim, and Button Sources

I use mainly vintage fabrics in my shop, but I do have fun designing lampshades with bold, contemporary fabrics as well. Below, you'll find a few of my favorites.

A.C. Moore
www.acmoore.com
A nationwide arts and crafts retailer.

Amy Butler Design
704-587-2841
www.amybutlerdesign.com
Look for her designs online and at local retailers.

Calico Corners
800-213-6366
www.calicocorners.com
A nationwide design retailer. Their mid-weight to lightweight fabrics are ideal for lampshade making. They also carry a large selection of trims.

Heather Bailey
877-872-7492
www.heatherbaileystore.com
I have used Heather's fabrics on the Cool Cottage Flowers Shade (page 60) and on the Electrified Kerosene Lamp (page 147). Heather's fabrics are manufactured and sold by FreeSpirit (www.freespiritfabric.com).

Fabric.com
888-455-2940
www.fabric.com
I love the European linen available through Fabric.com; it is affordable and of nice quality. I often shop here for quilt fabrics, too. They also carry a selection of FreeSpirit fabrics.

Flights of Fancy
800-530-8745
www.flightsoffancyboutique.com
Flights of Fancy is a great place to shop for a wide variety of new trims.

Jo-Ann Fabric and Craft Stores
www.joann.com
This nationwide retailer is a good source for scissors, trims, and notions. They also carry a selection of premade adhesive lampshades.

Kristine Tibbetts
678-947-1514 from October through April
978-544-2422 from April through October
www.buttonlady.net
Kristine sells buttons and aprons galore. Most recently, I bought curtain pushpins from her, perfect for making Vintage Pushpin Finials (page 150).

Michaels
www.michaels.com
A nationwide arts and crafts retailer.

Nifty Thrifty Dry Goods
401-246-0863
www.niftythriftydrygoods.com
Susan Gower, proprietor of Nifty Thrifty Dry Goods, has the most amazing selection of ribbons you'll ever see. I always go to Susan's booth at the Brimfield Flea Market (page 159).

QuiltHome.com
509-684-9000
www.quilthome.com
A great online source for those of us who live in the country!

Sis Boom by Jennifer Paganelli
www.sisboom.com
Sis Boom fabrics are such a joy to mix and match. Designer Jennifer Paganelli's fabrics are part of FreeSpirit's collection of fabrics (www.freespiritfabric.com) and are available at fabric and quilting stores throughout the country and online.

The Store Across the Street
64 West 38th Street
New York, NY 10018
212-354-1242
www.tinseltrading.com
A great shop from Tinsel Trading.

Susan Sargent Designs
3609 Main Street
Manchester, VT 05254
800-245-4767
www.susansargent.com
Susan's fabrics always seem to incorporate fun colors—perfect for lampshades. I used Susan's Dalia Toss Sungold pattern in the Funky Drum Shade (page 22).

Tinsel Trading Company
1 West 37th Street
New York, NY 10018
212-730-1030
www.tinseltrading.com
I have used many a trim from Tinsel Trading. They have a tiny shop in New York City and a great website.

Vintage Textiles, Fabrics, Trims, and Buttons

Many of the project fabrics are treasures I have found at antiques or vintage shops, flea markets, antiques shows, or online websites. Here I have included my favorite vintage textile sources. I am sure you will find your own favorites to add to my list! Some of the dealers listed sell only on their websites; other dealers have limited web presence and prefer to deal directly with the public at shows and flea markets.

Carlson & Stevenson Antiques and Art
802-362-3668
www.carlsonandstevenson.com
Phyllis Carlson is available by appointment in Manchester Center, Vermont, and at shows around the country.

French-Treasures.com
www.french-treasures.com
Carol Wood's website is part of my biweekly web crawl. She sells French fabrics, always a favorite in my shop.

Corning Stitch Works
15 West Market Street
Corning, NY 14830
607-377-5376
www.corningstitchworks.com
Maureen Jordan is a lampshade friend. She took one of my classes and sells great funky textiles at the Sturbridge textile show (page 158) as well as her vintage shop in Corning, New York.

Dusty's Vintage Linens
413-237-4467
Michele Piccolo and Lori Christian, proprietors, have lots of bright vintage tablecloths like the one used in the 1950s Kitchen Tablecloth Shade (page 101). They sell at the Brimfield Flea Market and at markets around the country and are a good source for linen, buttons, trims, and tablecloths.

Em's Heart Antique Linens
864-430-0372
www.emsheart.com
It's always fun to meet fellow textile addicts. Lynn Adams has a thorough website for vintage textiles.

Gandia-Todd Antiques
802-348-6603
These Vermont textile dealers show at many antique shows throughout New England.

Mairinger's Antiques
4473 Hurst Road
Altamont, NY 12009
518-861-5085
These dealers have gorgeous white linens, all ironed and clean. They are always generous with textile knowledge and show their wares throughout New England and New York.

Oldthreads Antique Textiles
716-557-2452
eBay seller: oldthreads
Lucy Jakubowski is a reliable dealer with great stuff.

Perennials Antiques
802-867-4189
www.perennialsantiques.com
Nancy Hagan shows at antiques shows in New England and Florida. A great source for transferware pottery and textiles.

Ruins
949-497-1085
www.ruins-ca.com
Lisa Genesta has an amazing collection of vintage treasures.

Susan Simon
212-663-5318
Though Susan is typically available only by appointment, you can catch her at shows around the country, including the Sturbridge vintage textile show (page 158).

The Textile Trunk
www.textiletrunk.com
eBay seller: loodylady
Wendy Lewis was an eBay friend and is now almost a Vermont neighbor. She heads to Europe several times a year and sells her stuff online.

Vintage and Antique Textiles
538 Main Street (Route 20)
Sturbridge, MA 01518
800-225-9406
www.vintageandantiquetextiles.com
Barbara Wright's shop is always worth a visit when I'm in Sturbridge.

Wendy J. Christie
717-336-0998
Wendy specializes in early homespun cottons and linens, especially nineteenth-century rural American cloth and clothing. I met Wendy at the Heart of the Mart textile tent at the Brimfield Flea Market (page 159).

Wiswall House Antiques
28 Wiswall Road
Durham, NH 03824
603-659-5106
www.wiswallhouseantiques.com
This antique shop's booth is always full of surprises. The owners travel to many shows in New England.

Lamps

Though you'll undoubtedly find stores near you for creating lamps, I've included a few of my favorite Vermont and New England lamp makers and shops here to get you started.

Authentic Designs
The Mill Road
West Rupert, VT 05776
800-844-9416
www.authenticdesigns.com
Michael and Maria Krauss's company is a designer's source for handsome turn-of-the-century lighting.

Gallery 103
Route 103
Chester, VT 05143
802-875-7400
www.gallery103.com
Stop by Elise and Payne Junker's Gallery 103 for wrought-iron lamps and Vermont crafts.

Hubbardton Forge
802-468-3090
www.vtforge.com
I've been shopping with this company since it started out in a barn with only wrought-iron floor lamps. Now, it's a nationwide company. You'll also find their wares in local lighting stores.

Island Granite Works
207-215-2877
www.islandgraniteworks.com
This store carries Maine rock lamps—a lamp that everyone seems to love, regardless of their decorating style.

Nantucket Lightshop
9 Sparks Avenue
Nantucket, MA 02554
508-228-6633
www.nantucketlightshop.com
You'll find my handcrafted lampshades here at Luann Martello Burton's shop, as well as a host of other lamps and shades.

Simon Pearce Glass
The Mill at Quechee
1760 Quechee Main Street
Quechee, VT 05059
800-774-5277
www.simonpearce.com
Over the years, I have made many a shade for the handsome hand-blown glass of the Simon Pearce glass studio, which also has stores nationwide.

A Lampshade Lady Road Trip in Search of Fabrics, Trims, and Lamps

I have included a few of my favorite antiquing and flea-marketing spots in New England, but no doubt you have your favorites near your home. To see a listing of flea markets throughout the country, check out www.keysfleamarket.com. For a complete listing of antique shows, go to www.maineantiquedigest.com.

Alice Peck Memorial Hospital Auxiliary Annual Spring and Fall Show Antique Show
Last Sunday in March and first Sunday in November
Lebanon, NH
207-882-6302

Antiques in Vermont Show
Riley Rink at Hunter Park
410 Hunter Park Road
Manchester Center, VT 05255
First Sunday in October

Sturbridge Antique Textile and Fashion Show
Monday of Brimfield Week, May, July, and September
Route 20
Sturbridge, MA 01566
207-439-2332
www.vintagefashionandtextileshow.com

Bromley Mountain Antique Show
First weekend in October
Bromley Base Lodge
Route 11
Peru, VT 05152
802-885-3705

Dorset Antiques Festival
(alternates every other year with the Hildene Antiques Show in Manchester Village, VT)
Village Green off Route 30N
Dorset, VT 05251
Saturday in early July; 10 a.m.–4 p.m.
207-767-3967
www.forbesandturner.com

Elephant's Trunk Country Flea Market
Route 7
New Milford, CT 06776
April–December; Sundays
508-896-1975
www.etflea.com

Farmington Antiques Weekend
152 Town Farm Road
Farmington, CT 06032
June and August; Saturday: 8 a.m.–5 p.m., Sunday: 10 a.m.–5 p.m.
317-598-0012
www.farmingtonantiquesweekend.com

Green Mountain Antiques Show
End of July
Union Arena
496 Woodstock Road
Woodstock, VT 05091
802-484-5942

Maine Antiques Festival
Union Fairgrounds
Fairgrounds Road off Route 17
Union, ME 04862
August; Saturday: 9 a.m.–5 p.m., Sunday: 9 a.m.–4 p.m.
207-221-3108
www.maineantiquefest.com

Montsweag Flea Market
Route 1 and Mountain Road
Woolwich, ME 04579
June–October; Wednesday: 5:30 a.m.–1:30 p.m.; antiques only, Saturday and Sunday: 6:30 a.m.–4:30 p.m.
207-443-2809
www.montsweagfleamarket.com

The Original Newfane Flea Market
Route 30
Newfane, VT 05345
Every Sunday: 6 a.m.
802-365-7771

Stormville Airport Antique Show and Flea Market
428 Route 216
Stormville, NY 12582
845-221-6561
www.stormvilleairportfleamarket
.com

Todd Farm Flea Market
303 Main Street
Rowley, MA 01969
April–November; Sundays, 5 a.m.–
3 p.m.
978-948-3300
www.toddfarm.com

Washington County Antique Fair and Flea Market
Washington County Fairgrounds
Route 29
Greenwich, NY 12834
First weekend in May and August;
Saturday: 8 a.m.–6 p.m., Sunday:
9 a.m.–5 p.m

Brimfield Antique and Flea Market Shows
Route 20
Brimfield, MA 01010
www.brimfield.com
May, July, and September; admission charge at some shows
Twenty different markets are set up within walking distance of one another during Brimfield Week. There are staggered opening days and hours, so be sure to check websites. Brimfield is just down the road from Sturbridge; I like to go to the Textile Show there on Monday, and then the flea markets start on Tuesday of Brimfield Week.

A few of my stops at the Brimfield Flea Market, all along Route 20

Central Park Antique Show
413-596-9257
www.brimfieldcentralpark.com

Heart of the Mart
413-245-9556
www.brimfield-hotm.com

Hertan's Antique Shows
860-763-3760
www.hertansbrimfield.com

J&J Promotions
413-245-3436
www.jandj-brimfield.com

May's Antique Market
413-245-9271
www.maysbrimfield.com

New England Motel Antique and Collectible Show
508-347-2179
www.antiques-brimfield.com

Quaker Acres Antique Shows
413-245-6185

Acknowledgments

I consider myself lucky to be one of "the lampshade ladies." My gratitude goes to Rosalie Smith and Elsa Waller, talented fiber artists and generous teachers, and to Jackie Rose, Susan Sargent, Poppy Gall, Jennifer Ellsworth, Dawn Pliner, Jackie Lappen, Scarlett Duncan, Patti Wieser, Elizabeth Cooper, Judy Pascal, Judy Lentz, Bethane Elion, Janno Gay, and Philippa Katz for their entrepreneurial inspiration. I also give great thanks to friend Jennifer Pagnolli for her colorful cotton fabrics.

I will be forever thankful for the friendship with my agent Angela Miller. Years ago Angela casually mentioned, "You should do a book someday," and I thought she was joking. . . . Wicked big thanks go to Kathleen Hackett, my co-author, for helping me find the confidence and skills to carry on, and to photographers Ryan Benji and George Bouret and their assistants Katie and Andrew. Thanks for the "Rick Rack" laughs and always getting those darn lampshades straight. Thank you to friends Vivian Weil, Peter Moore, Kristiane Kristianesen, and Ellen Adler for letting me into your wonderful homes for a day of photography.

Many thanks to the team at Potter Craft, especially to my editor Melissa Bonventre for her faith in this book. Thanks, also, to Rosy Ngo, Erica Smith, Betty Wong, Thom O'Hearn, Courtney Conroy, Jen Graham, and Rebecca Behan for helping me through the amazing book process. Thanks go to La Tricia Watford and Chi Ling Moy for the superb design.

Thank you to my husband Carson for his loving support, great meals, and for keeping me going each day and sending me off to do it all over again through fifty projects. Many thanks to Duncan, my son, for helping me with my computer questions and doling out big hugs. Lastly, thanks to my parents, Barbara and Alden Sawyer, for their support throughout the years, all of our fun craft projects with Andy and Mom, the ice candles, the pinecones, the taffy, the trips to Beacon Way for fabric, and of course all the country auctions—as long as the hot dogs and doughnuts held out.

Index